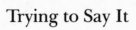

Trying to Say It

POETS ON POETRY · Donald Hall, General Editor

Philip Booth

Trying to Say It

OUTLOOKS AND INSIGHTS

ON HOW POEMS
HAPPEN

Ann Arbor
THE UNIVERSITY OF MICHIGAN PRESS

1999   1998   1997   1996   4   3   2   1

A CIP catalog record for this book is available from the British Library.

Library of Congress Cataloging-in-Publication Data

Booth, Philip E.
    Trying to say it : outlooks and insights on how poems happen /
Philip Booth.
        p.   cm. — (Poets on Poetry)
    ISBN 0-472-09586-2 (hardcover : alk. paper).—
ISBN 0-472-06586-6 (pbk. : alk. paper)
    1. Booth, Philip E.—Authorship.   2. Poets, American—20th
century—Biography.   3. Poetry—Authorship.   4. Poetics.
I. Title.
PS3503.0532Z475   1996
811'.54—dc20   96-11039
                                                                      CIP

For two librarians given
to words as well as books

Patricia Fowler
of the Witherle Memorial Library
in Castine

and

Philip Cronenwett
of the Dartmouth College Library
in Hanover,

in whose illimitable buildings
I long ago began to grow up

Contents

Distances/Shallows/Deeps

*Field Notes from an East-Facing Window at the
Cold End of a Long Maine Winter*

Nature, outside the window on this last Sunday in April, is an
East wind full of wet snow. And a cedar windbreak full of
newly arrived birds. In quick forays and flocked retreats they
pillage the final installment of millet and sunflower seed that
fills the feeder I hung last Thanksgiving on a wire stretched
across the warm corner between woodshed and house. No
sign of yesterday's pine siskins and mourning doves, but a
pair of cardinals in the appletree. Song sparrows and white-
throats, winter-dull goldfinches, chickadees, and juncos on
the feeder shelf. And cowbirds and redwings and grackles
tracking the snow under the feeder. Where yesterday's side-
yard robins have gone to shelter only the robins know.

❧

Nature doesn't have to be wilderness to be wild or be natural:
But wilderness, whether Arctic tundra or rain forest, is the
prime measure against which all other realms of Nature are
scaled, and on which they depend. When Thoreau claimed
"In wildness is the preservation of the world" he was intuiting
what has become prime ecological theory.

❧

Without Zero Population Growth, the concept of Forever Wild
can only seem ironic. But Nature cannot, we think, conceive of

From *The Ohio Review* Art and Nature issue no. 49 (winter 1993): 7–26.

concepts, as we believe we do. Now that Art has mostly grown beyond anthropomorphizing Nature, Nature no more needs our superimposition of a concept like irony than she needs more acid rain.

Rule One: *There is no irony in Nature.*

&

Some of us yearn for more B-2 bombers. Some of us yearn for Art. Some of us yearn for whatever century it was when humankind had invented sufficient machines, or imported enough slaves, to enable such leisure as allowed the more fortunate to pursue *their* search for God-in-Nature. Intimations of such profound transcendence were often felt where mountains were especially high, and their sublimity was then translated into Art. In, it is worth recalling, *all* civilizations.

Now, apparently envying or forgetting all of the above, we fly across oceans to ski great mountains deeply gashed by clear-cut trails and by the routes of chairlifts and cablecars that carry us to great heights, often with restaurants on top. From which, often on man-made snow, we let gravity return us to the valleys.

&

The trouble with Nature is us. The trouble with us is us.

&

We used to talk about good soil. Or about a good stand of trees. Or simply good land. Now we talk about property.

&

Today's weekend mail brings home its toll: glossy catalogs from L. L. Bean, The Nature Company, Orvis, Smith & Hawken, and Patagonia, with their splendidly functional inner- and outerwear, made from chemical fibers. And a multifold flyer from Mountain Travel, which will take you climbing in Patagonia, trekking in Nepal, walking in the Pyrenees, or rafting in China. All for a price. Not to mention the cost of whatever trees were felled for such glossy paper.

The human cost of such nonstop catalogs is equally obvious

in other kinds of envelopes: bids to support the American Indian College Fund, Planned Parenthood, Nature Conservancy, The United Negro College Fund, American Farmland Trust, American Cancer Society, Conservation Law Foundation, and Greenpeace. Except for two letters from poets, and one from a Texas daughter, there's not a piece of this mail that doesn't directly relate to the economic, and thus political, relationship between human nature and Nature. I'm trying to work, to let myself imagine, to get myself down to a poem. But it's already high noon. Where did the morning go?

ₐ

The rich grow richer: the planet gets poorer, the poor die terribly slowly.

ₐ

Nature is Nature, as Art is Art, primarily in the eye of the beholder. One decides, by degrees, how high or low on the scale a wild animal or a painting may be, depending on where one sees one's self standing on whatever stairway or hillside. A wolf is to a sheepdog, one might think, as the Adirondack wilderness is to Central Park. But in its own context Central Park seems wonderfully part of Nature, even as it was when that part of the Park now called Sheep Meadow was a meadow full of sheep. The Adirondacks (however full of coyotes and black bear) are a landscape less wild than Denali National Park, which is more or less wild than the North Slope, as long as that remote barrenness is inhabited by caribou and wolves rather than oil rigs, and as long as the Denali grizzlies don't get tamed by tourists. And as for Central Park's hierarchical standing as Nature (or civilization): amid an often uncivilized city, it's tempting to ask—thinking of Frederick Law Olmstead on an April morning when the Park surrounds its walkers and joggers with greening, blossoming, and birdsong—if landscaping is not, in itself, a considerable Art.

ₐ

On a smaller scale, a slate plaque bolted into a small cliff in a public garden on the high east side of Northeast Harbor on Mount Desert Island:

CHARLES KENNETH SAVAGE
1903–1979

Designer of Thuya Garden and its gate. Artist in landscaping and woodcarving. Lover of books. Public minded citizen in community and government. Conserver of ledges trees slopes for our delight.

❧

On whatever scale, the relationship between Nature and Art often looks from ground-level like a can of worms. The worms are, by any measure, marvels of Nature. But the can, much as Pop Art might like to see it as Stevens saw his jar in Tennessee, is a measure of utility rather than imagination. The worms don't need the can. No matter what it contains or what its exterior advertises, the can isn't Art. The can is simply one more item of humankind's low-tech wastefulness: maybe returnable, but unlike worms or us, not biodegradable.

❧

To match the LOVE IT OR LEAVE IT chauvinism recently generated by what used to be called brush-fire wars, it's a wonder that our president (Bush, still, as I write) doesn't further promote the frontier mentality of his ecological theories with the equally inviting LOVE IT AND LEAVE IT. Against which such powerful idea we Spotted Owl freaks are left with the presumably comforting directive of the plastic sticker LOVE YOUR MOTHER, often displayed on the rear bumpers of Volvo liberals.

❧

Jeffers wrote "I'd sooner, except the penalties, kill a man than a hawk." When, long later, the U.S. Postal Service gave him a posthumous stamp, the posters advertising the stamp quoted from another Jeffers poem: "One sees both ways, / And listens to the splendor of God, / The exact poet."

❧

In courts of law, testifying to tell the truth, we swear with one hand raised toward the ceiling, and the other hand on top of the Bible on which we base, or claim to base, much of Western

Civilization. For some considerable centuries we have believed, and literally made history out of, the Bible's first-chapter claim that God gave man great powers over Nature. His famous ruling, that we have "dominion over the fish of the sea, and over the fowl of the air, and over all the earth, and over every creeping thing that creepeth upon the earth," has only now, toward the end of the Twentieth Century, finally begun to creep up on us.

ಸಿ

Us being humankind. Nature being all of physical creation that is not us. Which is at least to say Earth, all that is animal, vegetable, mineral, that still inhabits, with us, the World, the civilization of which is apparently of our own making, and includes all Art. Whatever else Art is, it's by definition other than Nature. We ought to know: we, since Adam, have been the definition makers.

ಸಿ

My surest contact with both the planet and my daylight self is walking its ground foot by foot. Daily, both early and late.

ಸಿ

When I first read the preface to *Arctic Dreams,* and found Barry Lopez recalling a summer evening when he came down from a Brooks Range ridge to walk among nesting birds on the tundra, and found himself bowing to their fecund presence, their vulnerability, their courage, I knew I was in the presence of a man who was reporting back to my local dailiness a dream of where I had never been. Yet within my own psychic and geographic range I, too, have for years nodded my admiration to birds defending their territory. And on local shores, near the Equinox, when plovers and peeps in mid-migration are feeding at the ebb-tide's edge, I have seen what Lopez stunningly knows as a North light that "comes down over the land like breath, like breathing."

Sailing a small boat out into the bay in that same season, I now and then touch the long bill of my cap to salute an Arctic tern, knowing that his sleek head contains a navigation system which will take him across the Atlantic, and down the African coast, and out into the Antarctic Ocean before he flies back (a round trip of some twenty-thousand miles) to fish these waters again.

All such engaging moments are a primal joy: I'm being my solo self in sudden company with creatures who inhabit air or water in ways I cannot, creatures in whose presence I feel rather than think, being charged by the presence of their otherness to be in myself more alive.

ò.

What's atavistic in us wants contact with our natural origins. What's humanly imaginative in us wants to see not mere reproductions of great paintings, but to be in the presence of the original brushstrokes. The originality which informed a painting's creation presents its very being to our being us. And may well, if the painting's a landscape, revise our own view of Nature. My own sense of Maine islands demonstrably changed after I'd seen some of Marin's Deer Isle originals.

ò.

Auden's "Musée des Beaux Arts" and Jarrell's "The Old and the New Masters," read as a pair in that sequence, make for a fine Short Course in Perspective. Maybe, this side of photographs taken of Earth from Space, *the* Short Course in Perspective. Or perspective*s,* both spacial and, as Jarrell makes clear, temporal.

ò.

Bierstadt, Fitz Hugh Lane, Winslow Homer, Andrew Wyeth, and Marin, each to his own eye, time, and place, painted a stream I once fished in, the town in which I grew up and the house I still live in, seas I still fear, windows my heart has looked out from, and islands to which I still sail. I have both their images and mine, their Art and my own history in mind as I am, this moment, writing. Looking out the window at topography Lane painted a hundred and forty-some years ago, I too am immersed in my time: the time of my life as well as the end of what I was schooled to think of as a specific entity called the Twentieth Century. The light is no longer as pellucid as Lane painted it to be, now that a West wind brings us standard-brand fall-out from places where industry reigns.

è

Mostly after-the-fact, we tend to classify visual art more often in temporal terms than in spacial. Ionian, yes, all that; and not forgetting High Renaissance or Low Renaissance. But more commonly Pre-Raphaelite or Post-Modern or fin-de-siècle or Modern. But the basic aesthetic fact is that all Art is Post-Edenic.

è

All Art, even Kindergarten Art, whether finger-painting or drumming, is human nature's response to human nature and/or Nature. So is human language, our most basic response to what is about us. As witness the word *kindergarten*.

è

Or, long after kindergarten, consider how we yearn for, or fear, *prescience*. Especially at this far end of a technological century, only the first two years of which were, literally, pre-*flight*.

è

We yearned, for centuries before ours, for wings. All over the world. Now, in barely ninety years, aviation has exponentially changed our senses of distance and time; it has accelerated our lives in ways that, as we now defensively say, decontextualize them from self-defining places. Some days we long to fly over the Grand Canyon, or even down into it, for a new view. Some days we fear our next flight into O'Hare, an airport named for a WW II Navy fighter pilot who, like Icarus, finally fell into the sea.

è

I'm up, sometime around three, to answer what used to be called "Nature's call." And there's old Arcturus out the East window, hanging a little higher in the bare elm, and more to the West, than where Orion hung out around Hallowe'en. Awake again after five, I see sun coming behind an offshore cloud-bank. The barometer inside my study window is up to 1005, the thermometer outside at just 34°. I'll listen to NOAA weather while I shave; if anybody in my family is flying, I'm likely to watch Aviation Weather on TV. Maybe glance at whatever blizzards, droughts, or earthquakes are being felt in Milwaukee, the Napa Valley, or Peru. But nobody else's weathers have the impact of weathers that come home to one's own life. Like the sixty-six hours when the Syracuse Blizzard of '66 marooned our North Eagle Village Road house, and the five of us in it, under sixty-six inches of snow. Or when, on March 2d of some other year, the snowmelt off Dry Hill flooded us to the tune of three inches over the slab to which that house was anchored. As Frost said in "Storm Fear," there are times when we doubt whether we have it in us to "save ourselves unaided."

ஜ

Calvin, in Watterson's "Calvin and Hobbes" comic strip, shows up in full color in today's *Bangor Daily News,* mad as hell about getting rained on when he wanted a sunny Sunday: He screams at the sky "Hey, are you listening?" The sky booms thunder, and Calvin rises to the challenge, his arms and mouth both wide: "It's man against the elements! Conscious being versus insentient Nature! My wits against your force. *We'll* see who triumphs!"

ஜ

What "we'll see" greatly depends on what kinds of Art we create. We humans have invented all kinds of ways to destroy Nature and ourselves, God knows. Or say God doesn't. How ironic it will be if we can't, or don't, create Art that not only authenticates our lives, but makes present *in* our lives such joy that we no longer need to destruct each other (and the great other, Nature) for want of imagination.

ஜ

Ground-level Lines Worth A Lifetime Of Standing On Hill-tops In Thunderstorms For:

These:

> The salt is on the briar rose,
> The fog is in the fir trees.

These:

> It was evening all afternoon.
> It was snowing
> And it was going to snow.

These:

> By the road to the contagious hospital
> under the surge of the blue
> mottled clouds driven from the
> northeast—a cold wind. Beyond, the
> waste of broad, muddy fields
> brown with dried weeds, standing and fallen . . .

These:

> The reeds give
> way to the
>
> wind and give
> the wind away

Eliot, Stevens, Williams, Ammons: a place, a time, a weather. Nature, humankind, Art.

ঌ

Thoreau (May 23, 1854): "We soon get through with Nature. She excites an expectation which she cannot satisfy. . . . Man *should be* the harp articulate."

ঌ

Hopkins: A Short Course in the Evolution of Ecology

#31   The world is charged with the grandeur of God.
         It will flame out, like the shining of shook foil . . .
            . . . .
         And for all this, nature is never spent . . .

#37   Glory be to God for dappled things—
           For skies of couple-colour as a brinded cow;
              For rose-moles all in stipple upon trout that swim . . .
            . . . .
           And áll trádes,   their gear and tackle and trim.

#43   (Binsey Poplars / felled 1879)

> Where we, even when we mean
>   To mend her we end her,
>   When we hew or delve:
>
> After-comers cannot guess the beauty been.
>   Ten or twelve, only ten or twelve
>   Strokes of havoc unselve
>   The sweet especial scene.

#56   What would the world be, once bereft
       Of wet and wildness? Let them be left,
       O let them be left, wildness and wet;
       Long live the weeds and the wilderness yet.

#58   Earth . . .

               . . . with no tongue to plead, no heart to feel.

                              ❧

In Camus' *The Fall* (1956), his first-person narrator's view of
the Zuider Zee from a dike on the island of Marken:

> Well, what do you think of it? Isn't it the most beautiful nega-
> tive landscape? Just see on the left that pile of ashes they call a
> dune here, the gray dike on the right, the livid beach at our
> feet, and in front of us, the sea the color of a weak-lye-solution
> with the vast sky reflecting the colorless waters. A soggy hell,
> indeed! Everything horizontal, no relief; space is colorless, and
> life dead. Is it not universal obliteration, everlasting nothing-
> ness made visible?

                              ❧

Against such nothingness, Greenpeace has given the world
twenty good years of (as they say) "Raising Hell." Which basi-
cally means human beings interposing their lives between Na-
ture and those other beings hellbent on killing whales, poison-
ing rivers and farmlands, incinerating toxics into the sky. And
so on. And on. Strange, how in many rural counties in this
country, a lot of people still talk about where they live as "the
old home place."

                              ❧

10

Life of any kind literally "takes place." Most of our classic assays of living with Nature begin by naming their place: *Walden, The Outermost House, Sand County Almanac, Pilgrim at Tinker Creek*. And *Arctic Dreams*, the subtitle of which defines an aspect of all these books as well as its own splendor: "Imagination and Desire / in a Northern Landscape." Before all else, *place* itself impresses whoever explores and observes it. And then self must explore both self and language in order to express what can be related, desired, even partially known. Living with Nature is opening one's self to a place full of all-we-are-not, where profoundly constant change does not accommodate to our human schedule or our presumptuous human priorities.

Still, Nature informs some part of our human nature whether we live and write in sight of Mt. Rainier or in midtown Manhattan. No matter where we experience being in place, we immerse in our deepest selves when we begin to write. It's from instinctive memory, from the wilderness of imagination, from a mindfulness forever wild, that Art starts.

٤

Art rarely invites instant gratification. Just as Art takes time to create, and undergoes all sorts of transformations and revisions in the process of being created, art needs to be responded to by countless re-seeings or re-hearings or re-readings. Art literally appreciates as we assimilate it into our lifetimes.

٤

Even when we think Art comes out of nowhere, Art comes out of everywhere, the everywhere we don't know until we begin to join words or chisel stone or fling paint. Art transforms us to the extent, and depth, that our lives have informed it.

٤

Art draws on Nature without invasion. The stars did not fall because Van Gogh swirled them in his mind's eye and gave his hand to paint what he felt he saw.

≈

From Nature (believe it or not), human nature creates (believe it or not) Art. From Nature, too, we humans invent technology, which is, in itself, less imaginative than either Science or Art. <u>Art and Science are slowly earned responses requiring consummate reflection.</u> Technology and Entertainment are more quickly contrived and more easily received. Worldwide, television is the great leveler: Technology spawning Entertainment.

≈

Since satellite technology has collapsed time/space to the extent of providing instantaneous transmission/reception from Berlin, Space, or L.A., we spend more and more time in the space in front of our television screen, looking at what television dictates that we see: what passes as entertainment, information, or sport. One of the passions of TV is not only to seduce us into buying what it dictates we should want, but to keep us watching TV rather than looking into our own lives. Which might mean freely conversing with someone else, or reading, or walking to a museum. Or even looking out the window for whatever Nature still exists.

≈

TV keeps us looking, looking, looking, as we press and press the remote to find out what we're missing. Nothing could be further from the jittery passivity of such channel-scanning than the people in Frost's poem who searchingly "look at the sea all day." Frost says flatly:

> They cannot look out far.
> They cannot look in deep.

Yet Frost greatly values, and is part of, "the watch they keep" over a Nature that is at once moving and incomprehensible. "In deep" and "out far" are, in Frost's work, the prime foci of his search for any outlook that might provide insight. Stopping by woods on a snowy evening, he finds himself choosing to keep familiar "promises" rather than succumb to woods that are temptingly "lovely" but ultimately "dark and deep."

In a longer poem, "The Star-Splitter," wondering "after all, where are we," he repeatedly looks through the telescope of a friend who bought it by burning "his house down for the fire insurance" in order, like Frost, to look out far, "To satisfy a lifelong curiosity / About our place among the infinities."

à

Everything we see on TV is an elsewhere, often a Nowhere designed to attract our envy and, thus, our dollar. Everything TV seductively or blatantly tries to sell us has already been bought and sold. Most of it is patently vicarious vacuity. TV both buys and sells two-dimensional space and an accelerated time full of time-outs. For all its spectacularly instantaneous excitements, it distorts our lives, and makes them more shallow than they often already are: it doesn't provide place, or give time, for reflection.

à

Einstein's saying that God is subtle rather than malicious has always troubled me. Malice I doubt, particularly in the same sentence with subtle. But anybody walking, or working, an upland woodlot in all four seasons can't help but sense the subtlety.

à

In the eight quick lines of "Nothing Gold Can Stay," Frost is midway between Wordsworth's ever diminishing sense of being able to "praise the day," and Roethke's attempt to re-entitle himself to such praise. Frost's observation that the "gold" of "Nature's first green" is "Her hardest hue to hold" raises such knowledge to considerable powers as he memorially recognizes that as "leaf subsides to leaf . . . / So Eden sank to grief" and "So dawn goes down to day."

Only the language of poetry or the alacrity of dance (which are closely related) can enact such recognition with such specific gravity.

à

A Dutch novelist, much travelled, writes me from Berlin, en route to Romania and Japan, that he thinks of my Maine rootedness in terms of "the Cistercian vow, *stabilitas loci*," which he says he half envies. But even as I half envy him, my choice, were there ever as much, would be in some further life to come back as a seaduck. Best of all as an Oldsquaw, my maleness darker during tundra summers, white during Maine winters when, afloat in my home harbor, I'd at will swim my wings underwater to fish deep for mussels or shrimp; and then surface again to chortle my call, knowing all the time I could fly.

໓

Admiring Annie Dillard's *Pilgrim at Tinker Creek,* Eudora Welty said that "A reader's heart must go out to a young writer with a sense of wonder so fearless and unbridled." True, over and over, with young writers in various genres: Gretel Ehrlich's autobiographical *The Solace of Open Spaces.* Even younger, Gabrielle Ladd, who died in a plane crash before her first twenty poems were published as *The Dark Island.* Brook Haxton's *Dominion.* And, and, and. . . . But in us all, where does the wonder go?

We grow to know too much we cannot bear to feel.

໓

Thoreau's inclination to travel much in Concord rather than transport himself "to count the cats in Zanzibar" takes on exponential ironies in the 1990s: Our Decade of Quantification.

໓

Never mind that "the bottom line" has become our national metaphor. Any common language now either tells or sells. Even basic measures have so lost meaning that firewood sold by the cord in Upstate New York proves, on delivery, not to stack out to $4' \times 8' \times 4'$, but to measure $4' \times 8' \times 2'$, which the seller, if pressed, will acknowledge is, yes, "a face cord."

໓

Why aren't I writing more about Nature, or Art? About their interrelation? Because the foreground static of corrupt language and inane quantification interferes with imagination.

Never mind the suppertime stock market index or the evening's instant batting averages, or rushing yards gained, or number of baskets against a particular opponent; simply check the statistics which emblazon every day's *USA Today.* The numbers range from the absurd to the obscene: from the front-page graph of the percentage of youth-size as against full-size tennis racquets recently sold, to figures straight from Washington that deny war-costs and miscount the homeless.

ﻬ

The fin-de-millennium scientist-poets are many and remarkable, not least Fritjof Capra, Lewis Thomas, Stephen Jay Gould, Stephen Hawking, Timothy Ferris. Each deserves such attentive reading as an old man I once knew in Bradford, Vermont, gave to Eddington's classic *Space, Time, and Gravitation* some seventy years ago.

I've read, or tried to read, all of the above. But I too often stall out on chapters beyond my capacity for numbers, scientific theory, and abstraction. Even books with such self-consciously tempting titles as *The Dancing Wu Li Masters* and *The Search for Schrödinger's Cat* confound my wish to search and, indeed, to dance. Kant's *Prolegomena to Any Future Metaphysics* is, to my mind, even more impenetrable; and I'm even unable to assimilate Koestenbaum's introduction to Husserl's *Paris Lectures,* much less grasp the lectures themselves. I read three pages, underlining, making marginal notes, and retreat; and the next night start all over again with total astonishment at all I've already failed to remember.

Chaotic as life, mind, world, and universe seem sometimes to be, I'm still unable to sustain Prigogine's *Order Out of Chaos.* With Teilhard de Chardin I do somewhat better, but I basically need the specificities of ground-level immediacy and perception that are closer to wherever my own head seems daily to be. My own nature can happily comprehend, in a more pedestrian book called *My Weeds,* Sarah Stern's lucent chapter on how bindweed multiplies and how garlic, in anybody's backyard garden, clones.

ﻬ

Scale defines Art, and any particular work of Art, as surely as Nature is the measure on which our sense of scale is based. Somewhere between subatomic particles and the outermost realms of the cosmos, here are we humans (indeed created from both realms), both artists and scientists, trying on one small planet to relate to each other how we each (and all) do or don't relate to either everything or nothing. Insofar as each of us is demonstrably other than each other, those of us who are artists of one kind or another instinctively search—as photographers more rationally and specifically do—for something like a lens of the particular focal length which best suits our sense of seeing what is about us, and what we are about.

For us poets, in relating what we're about (and perhaps what the all is about), the scale of our saying relates to the measure of the line we intuitively hear as we write. Dickinson's line, as a familiar for instance, in contrast to Whitman's. But what any artist draws, dances, sings, composes, sculpts, writes, depends on the scale of her or his life, including such *choice* of scale as goes well beyond genetic predilection. I come back and back to my certain sense that it's only as part of the total procession of all of Nature's (and thus history's) equinoxes that we happen to live our lives: that in the process of living those lives we recapitulate phylogeny; and that in the process of creating Art as part of our relation to past and present, our Art is a deepening and furthering of Creation itself.

ᴥ

The long V of the Bay I sail is some 15,000 years deep. Gouged and widened then by the Wisconsin ice-sheet, which left scars of its passage on the granitic slopes of small mountains it scraped and scoured, its glacial valley was more lately drowned by polar ice-melt, the sea so risen that the scarred slabs of granite became the shorelines of the hundred islands among which I sail. Tacking between islands in both time-present and geologic time, playing the wind, watching eiders, listening to loons and island whitethroats from a boat moving on constantly changing sea-levels and periodic tides, I'm given perspectives both horizontal and vertical, perspectives constantly new. The landward horizons of the bay could well be those of Western Vermont or the Berkshires, were not the present coastal hills, and the scoured mountaintops, being redefined daily by Atlantic weathers. Between wind and water, I ride waves riding ocean swells, as those swells ride Labrador currents. All of which call my eye out to sea.

&

The great NASA photographs taken of Earth from the all-but-unimaginable realm of Space, marvellously gathered in *The Home Planet,* make for an abstract Art surpassing all previous colors and perspectives. Looked down to through hundreds of transparent miles and a scatter of fair-weather cumulus or streaked cirrus, the very nature of Earth has clearly given a whole generation of astronauts, of literally detached observers, a chance to rediscover their passionate attachment to the planet. Looking, from out far, far down to Rio Negro, to the Namib Desert, the Grand Canyon, the Indian Ocean, or the whole curved horizon beyond the East Coast of Somalia, the astronauts found themselves transcending all manner of human and historical boundaries. In languages as different as Vietnamese, Russian, Dutch, Romanian, Chinese, English, and Arabic, they variously wrote what translates from a Saudi observer's notebook as graphically universal: "The first day or so we all pointed to our countries. The third or fourth day we were pointing to our continents. By the fifth day we were aware of only one Earth."

&

Whether come from in deep, or arrived from immeasurable distance, the impulse to create Art is an active response to what we more passively sense as "real" events in "real" places in "real" time. Yet potentially as "timeless" as music, all Art creates its own place in our lives: the shock of recognition it gives our own imagination is in itself, like its very creation, a true event.

&

Frost, though he demonstrably knew, through poem after poem, how rarely Nature gives what we ask of her, yearned,

17

like most of us, on whatever scale of being, for what, in "The Most of It," he calls "counter-love, original response." In that poem his general sense of existential loneliness is specifically confirmed by the "mocking echo" of his own voice from some "tree-hidden cliff" across a lake. "Nothing ever came of what he cried" unless, in the immediate instance, it was the embodiment of "a great buck" that "powerfully appeared" to be swimming toward him, "pushing the crumpled water up ahead." But as the buck stumbles out into the underbrush in a conclusion which deeply confirms the poem's title, Frost enigmatically concludes "and that was all."

Enigmatic as the poem's conclusion is, the poem itself is, paradoxically, Frost's "original response" to an event in some part originally literal. Literal, that is, until it became the poem we now read, the poem to which—depending on our own experience and identification with Frost's yearning—we quite possibly return such "counter-love" as Frost could not sense in the specific Nature of the poem or, at large, in the universe. If, if, if we can open our inmost selves to experience the poem as a whole, the poem may in some way change our own sense of Nature, even as we are changed by each new reading. Any original work of art gives us what the continually original flux of Nature seldom provides. Here, the poet's creative vision (and revision in the process of writing) imaginatively enables us to read and reread: to repeatedly respond to an event that—should it so move us—might well inform, even transform, the rest of our unrestful lives.

ઢ

Waking from nightmares beyond midnight, submerged in the dark, I reach for my earphones, press the FM transistor switch, and am filled with a music that feels familiar but for which I have no name. Except as my mind registers chants that seem Latinate, I am in the presence of sounds that belong both to Nature and Art, to World and to Planet. Though less aleatory than the sounds of whales I have heard at sea, the conjunctive tones of music and voice move me as deeply as whalesong. I wildly think that whales would understand what I'm hearing. I am transported, totally immersed in sentience.

I am hearing aspects of myself and of my life which I never before heard: where there are voices, I do not understand words as such but hear a whole music that is, in its intervals, its crescendoes and diminuendoes, its instrumental and human voicings, a language wholly new. I wake again, or wake the more, to a new depth of feeling, and find myself weeping in the calm of great joy. I think of harbor seals with whose quizzically risen heads I have, from a boat, often conversed; I again hear the language of pilot whales translated through the hull of the boat in which I helped steer their confusion out of a local cove. I go back to deep sleep, my human nature fulfilled in whatever realm I have immediately been, a realm intermediary between what I now remember as a resurrection of thirteenth-century music and what I know of seals fishing, and seaducks drifting the dark tides a thousand yards east of this house: creatures beyond me feeling and sounding, barely resting, living lives which deeply touch mine, even as they live lives I can barely touch. And out beyond their lives, out over the tidal harbor, the bay with its coastal villages, the world of human lives whose music most of all moves me. "Lives," as I long ago wrote, "we barely know, lives / we keep wanting / to know."

Robert Lowell's Summers in Castine
Contact Prints, 1955–65

Except for the Smith's Mill picnic, which is one step out of clock time, this is a chronological strip of contact prints: views of Cal, a friendship, a decade, a place. To get back to how Cal affected me, and this peninsular village, I have fictionalized time present: the presumptive now *of a camera. Except for reviewing actual photographs, and the notes I took when Cal first looked at my poems, I have relied entirely on memory—memory checked with my wife Margaret, and with friends.*

As with any film left in a camera for years, there are, here, whole seasons left out; unexpectedly, there are two or three frames which exhibit their own sequence. What's missing, inevitably, is any sustained soundtrack: the power of Cal's talk, the gestures of Cal's voice, his hands' sprung rhythms, are partially here; I have tried to be as true as possible to who Cal was in these several—or eleven—summers. They became, finally, only an overlong August: the high stillness between McCarthyism and Vietnam.

There were further summers, larger talk, more poems; but fewer and fewer picnics. The world changed. And Castine, now, is almost as greatly changed by Cal's leaving as it was by his coming. I miss him immensely.

1

My first year downcountry, driving John Holmes back from the Gardner house in Brookline, where we've been invited to

From *Salmagundi* 37 (Spring 1977): 35–53.

meet Robert Lowell. The party is as big as the house, as casually elegant, to honor his homing from Iowa.

As we drive back across the river, John asks what I thought about Lowell. Isabella Gardner I met, yes; Donald Hall, yes; and more poets than I ever knew existed. But I have to tell John I didn't meet Robert Lowell. I would have remembered that sternly handsome young man peering down from the gallery of portraits in Oscar Williams' newest anthology. No, I somehow missed meeting him. But, as I tell John, I did have good talk with another Lowell about his coming to Maine—a great bear of a man with hornrimmed glasses who slumped darkly away from me in a tall Victorian chair.

"He must have been Lowell's brother," I tell John; "he said his name was Cal."

2

After we've read together at Brown, Cal's Tudor Ford ahead of Margaret and me at a Providence stoplight. Cal's head tipped down to the book he has just picked up from the seat beside him. His own poems. The light goes green, then yellow, then red again. The whole of Route 1 behind us, beginning to honk. But Cal, for minutes and minutes, keeps on reading.

3

Down over the Main Street knoll, the postoffice; and down below that—at the steep end of Main Street—the village drugstore, Ken's Market, the flagpole, the Town Wharf, and the sea.

Nothing has changed in the six years since I've been home for the summer. The same key hung in the hall still fits the same postoffice box. As I search through my take for rejections or an acceptance, I hear Cal's voice at the oak-framed postoffice window, asking Irene for mail for Lowell.

Cal seems to be as pleased to see me as I am to see him. He

says I must come down to the seaside Barn to "trade poems," the barn "behind the Brickyard House where we're staying." But I don't know his private names for his cousin's place, and he is too new here to be able to give exact directions. Never mind, I can find it. As already the mail has found Cal: I help him lug piles of publisher's and author's copies out to his Ford. In his blue buttondown and his bluejeans, Cal looks both like and unlike the poet I met in Boston. But his grin is entirely wide, the eyes behind his hornrims are glad.

Elizabeth and Cal *here.* Unlikely. For them, and for us. But what luck. For the whole rest of the summer.

4

Against sunset, against summer's end, against the prevailing sou'westerlies which stress and release even the peninsula's strongest elms, Cal plays tennis almost every afternoon at one of the two courts next to the High Road. The company at these late-afternoon sessions of round-robin doubles is socially elect. The voices are pure Eastern Shore, West Hartford, and Boston, but the talent is severely mixed: Cal wins one set with Janet Hughes, twenty years his senior, then loses a second set with Sally Austin, skilled and barely of age. His legs never get him to the right place on the court at the right moment, but he compensates by attacking the ball with all the immense strength of his upper body. His reflexes, if not always coordinated, are quick: even when his stroke flails he scores points with his running monologue—this particular game variously reminds him of Philip of Macedonia, his first wife, and Aristophanes. Elizabeth, exhausted after two sets, gangles on the sidelines under the cedars.

Cal is about to serve. Sweating hugely, he strips his shirt (violating the only club rule ever posted), and says, "This may make me as famous as René LaCoste. . . ." Wherever fame may reside, it will not reside in his service: he throws the ball too low, ducks from his knees to accommodate the failed altitude, pushes at the ball from too short an arc, and with great speed squashes it into his partner's left buttock. She smiles back wildly at Cal, and he invites everybody for supper.

Everything stops. Cal glances hugs at Elizabeth, and turns back happily to his tennis partners. "If you can't do that," he says, "at least come for drinks."

5

A northwest wind day. Large scale clarities. In spite of shut doors, the shoreside Barn where Cal writes (table, chair, type-writer, and cot set at the windows fronting Oakum Bay) is a barn too September-cold for long talk. Cal escorts me out to the lee wall of the Barn; we sit in sweetgrass, sun glinting up off the harbor.

After thanking me for introducing him to the bluejean jacket he's just beginning to wear from stiff to soft, Cal starts straight in on my manuscript. Depending on the quality of his interest, he turns slowly or quickly the pages he has had now for two days. Sometimes he reads aloud, his head tipped forward with total focus on the poem, then looks up at me over his glasses and smiles his reassurance: "That's what I like best—the sparse and accurate description." Then, his expression slightly pained, he says of another poem, ". . . but the resonance is too obvious." And, turning pages, he finds a lot to attack in a poem called "Red Brick": "too full of strained personification, too general, too shrill." He stops, lets up, smokes, and says I should read "say three poets for a month, maybe copying-out poems" to see what I can learn to use, to extend my range. "Empson for intellect. Marianne Moore for observation, Frost for how a poem gets organized."

Back again to the poems, he goes at them totally, liking "this rougher metric," dismissing that "intellectual indolence." He insists that all of the description, not just sections, be "as solid as the first part of *Life on the Mississippi,* or the crossing-the-river part of *As I Lay Dying.*" A lot of his touchstones are prose. But against the general dangers of "balsam pillow Maine," he again shifts to poetry; he wants to send me to

Arnold's shorter lines, "Tennyson rowing out to Catullus's island," Hardy's "narrative strength," or Wordsworth's simplicity in "Michael"; and "the 'thereness' of 'Tintern Abbey.'"

All this I half know but have never before heard. My one college writing course far behind me, I begin to understand that I am for the first time hearing a master teacher. I listen and listen, reminding myself that when I get home I must write myself notes about everything Cal is saying.

The sun is across apogee, the wind has calmed and come back from the south before Cal is done with me. If he withheld anything, I'm not sure I want to know what that anything is. I feel like the new boy taken out behind the gym by a Sixth Former, being told quietly that one isn't living up to the school's best traditions.

As we get up from the shingled barn wall and the sweetgrass, Cal shakes my hand. But it is neither congratulation nor goodbye; it is, rather, as if something new had begun. I walk along the harbor, and home up the hill, stunned by Cal's impact. Nobody before has ever cared so much for my poems: cared to criticize them so brilliantly, cared so to demand of them, even in parts so cared to praise them, as Cal has this day.

6

Annually now, like my native grandmother and his summer cousin before us, Cal and I have inherited being neighbors across a mid-village back pasture. It's still hard to put together the virtuosity of *Lord Weary's Castle* with the white clapboard Augusts we're beginning to share. There's never been question who is the senior poet. Nor whose territory Cal has moved to. I less want Cal's good wine than I want to hear him talk more about Hardy; I'm continually knocked over by the intensity of his intelligence. But Cal wants to hear the Maine voice in which I tell stories, or he wants to be taken sailing. To whatever experience I'm native, Cal is deferential, with innate Boston ease.

After supper in the Lowells' barn, that tall summerroom

Cal's Cousin Harriet made from the old ell back of her house on the Common, we have variously taken in dishes and come back in front of the fire. We've talked long, over wine, salad, and coffee. Now Cal has put Nadia Boulanger records on Harriet Winslow's old Magnavox; while the four of us listen, I find myself feeling that if there's another war this is the kind of civilization I'd want to remember. Or want to try to save.

Elizabeth's early to bed; Margaret has walked up the hill to let our babysitter go home. Cal's back to Hardy, and his ability to imply narrative. As we talk, I get to how circular Maine stories are. Remembering Cal's pleasure in Mace Eaton's seal story, I tell Cal about this noon on the wharf: Mace asking me if I'd been across the harbor for clams, then (literally, with his finger) ribbing me that "Clams'll makeyuh stemmy!" Cal laughs, catching the aphrodisiac implication but wanting me to repeat the metaphor in my own voice.

"Oh," he says, "*stemmy!* That's nearly Shakespearian. But you haven't taken me to meet Mace yet. . . ." Cal's hands dance in front of him in pure delight. "Let's do that *soon.*"

7

Chokey and fevered with a pharynx abscess, I've kept myself propped up in bed by rereading *War and Peace* for the best part of two days and the worst of two nights. This second night I dreamt the Battle of Borodino, with Cal cast as Pierre. After penicillin broke my abscess, and my fever, I woke in high relief: the battle was over. But even on this June morning the after-image sustains itself: Cal as Pierre.

8

On the waterfront here, even in the protective coloration of his bluejean jacket, Cal seems as vaguely outlandish as Pierre in his white suit.

A lot of Cal's energies blur when he can't verbally focus them. For matters simply practical, Cal has no native talent;

his natural frames of reference are as historical-literary as my dream. Even his most pedestrian associations are freestyle, full of verbal leaps, until they fall into some narrative play or pivot on a phrase or a word. For instance: *submarine.*

Today, over the Fourth, we traipse our conglomerate families down to the Town Wharf to visit the submarine that the Navy has sent in, and opened to the public for the day. The ladders are vertical, the passages narrow; our wives and daughters are variously gaped at or saved from hysterics by the incredibly young submariners in their Navy dress blues. After we've been guided the length of the submarine's innards, and have asked civilian questions about torpedoes and periscopes, we climb back topside, out into the gleam of the harbor. Cal turns to me with a question which must have preoccupied him for the whole dark length of our short tour. "Tell me," he says, his hands waving awkwardly down from the wharf to the submarine moored alongside, "are the men who sail that thing *Marines?*"

I explain. Cal shakes his huge head: "Oh, I should have *known* that." He is genuinely, if momentarily, embarrassed. But it is by just such associative leaps that some of Cal's best poems get written.

9

I submarined myself this summer, having taken Cal out sailing around the bell. As we came back into the harbor on a dying breeze, I asked Cal if he wanted to take the helm. He did, accompanied by improbable tales of his sailing in Padanaram as a boy. These somehow slid into a wonderfully funny story about sexual mores in Dubuque; a wonderfully funny story at which Margaret laughed more than I only because Cal was letting the boat gybe at will, all over the harbor. The air was too light to have these gyrations hurt the boat, but she was easily identifiable along the waterfront, and it hurt my pride to have her sailed badly in such public view. Aside from some suggestions, readily accepted by Cal, to head for this buoy, or that farm on the shore, I held in my frustrations until we neared the wharves. I mentioned the difficult set of the current, took back the helm from Cal, and buttonhooked up to our mooring. Margaret neatly picked up the pennant with the boathook, but then proceeded to cleat it with perhaps her right hand rather than her left. I jumped forward past Cal with all my frustrations vented on my wife, grabbed the pennant from her, cleated it the other way around, and stood quickly straight up, puffing angrily on my pipe. Next thing I knew I stepped one step smartly backwards, plunk into the harbor.

This event has become, variously embellished, a waterfront story which Cal likes even better than Mace Eaton stories. Tonight at dinner, with Fred and Andy Dupee up from the Brickyard House they've again been renting, and with the Wannings over from Blue Hill, Cal got me to tell Mace's seal story, then led me on to tell about falling overboard. My version ends with some slight face-saving: I went down sucking my pipe and surfaced with the pipe still clamped in my jaw.

"Oh," Cal roars to everybody, "that's only a *tenth* of it. He tells a story with perfect pitch for Maine accent, but . . ." Cal all but explodes with delight at having so set me up. "But aboard his boat he's an absolute Ahab!"

Cal's no Ahab, afloat or ashore. But at dinnerparties he's no Pierre, either. Elizabeth's dinners in the summerroom are done with a grace that makes them seem easy. And everybody is, in fact, greatly at ease. Including Cal. But he plays a dinnerparty at the pitch at which he plays tennis. Given an audience of more than one, Cal turns conversation into his best competitive sport.

Cal is immensely knowing in all sorts of worlds beyond Castine: poetry, politics, women—in every possible permutation and combination. He has many appetites, but the surest of these is for talk. Talk at the level he must have exchanged with Randall Jarrell, and with Delmore. But we here are, at best, intermediates to Cal's expertise. Cal serves with high wit; his wild intelligence never misses an opportunity to score. The dinner table is, for him, centercourt at Longwood. As if in total relief from writing, or from shop talk, Cal tries every shot in the book: dropshot, lob, slam. There are few long rallies; it is almost impossible to drive Cal back to some conversational baseline. But dinnerparties, supperparties, are stunning games of intelligence at play, every exchange ending and never ending in strokes of quick victory or happy collapse.

10

Cruising friends of ours made port late this afternoon, downeast a day early on steady southerlies. By quick arrangement, we took them in tow to the Lowells' house for that rarest Lowell event: a cocktail party. A lot of people, but even among them the cruising Blacks are literally outstanding: Carol is gracefully rigged, Peter is about as tall as the mast of their French sloop. Asked today what he does when he isn't cruising, Peter said, "I make money. I don't see much other reason for working."

In his own old Irish tweed jacket and khakis, Cal listened diffidently to Peter's tailored aplomb; but once they meet, Cal is immensely pleased to know that Peter knows his poems. Peter is expert in everything: international shipping, skippering, shooting tigers, watercolors, making fish chowder, cabinet making, and knowing how to spend old money gracefully. Cal sees all this at a glance; Peter is deeply Boston. Yet only after almost everybody has left the summerroom, and we're saying goodbyes and thanks, does Cal speak to Peter his recognition.

"Didn't you go to Noble's? And before that didn't you live near the Ameses?"

Peter nods his surprise.

Cal, again: "I think your aunt brought you to Revere Street once. . . ."

Peter does not remember.

". . . You're the boy my mother always tried to get me to play with." Cal's eyes blink hugely, he ducks his head repeatedly, like a zoo bird, in spondaic assent to his earliest memories. "She thought that if we played together a lot I'd be more like you." His left hand begins a circular apology. "And rather less like me. . . ."

Cal grins his widest grin. Peter roars. Boston is intact.

Life Studies has made Cal famous. Even here. Auden's claim that "poetry makes nothing happen" to the contrary, "our fairy decorator" has already left town. *Post hoc,* maybe *propter hoc.*

"Skunk Hour" isn't my favorite life study (though I feel the vested interest of having helped Cal get his yawl down from twelve knots in draft to a more realistic nine), but it's the only poem I ever heard talked about on any Main Street. And it has mightily confounded the elderly Boston ladies who here live out their handsomely furnished lives. Cal is still "Bobby" to some of them, who knew his mother; they indeed know something of his personal history. Little or much as they may understand of "Skunk Hour," what troubles them is its tone: they feel threatened by what they take in the poem to be "Bobby's not liking it here." It's difficult, if not impossible, to say simply that—save for weathers of flat depression, hanging in like day after day of fog—Cal has mostly been well here, that he has written well here, that he is generally happy here, and that "Skunk Hour" is about more than a man named Lowell or a town named Castine. How possibly say to the Boston ladies, or anybody else local, that Cal's poems (as Stevens says of his "Comedian . . .") "make / Of his own fate an instance of all fate."

After Cal read last year to benefit the community hospital, he seemed stranger than ever to the people who went, mostly, out of obligation or curiosity. The school gym was barren, and too hot; the acoustics were terrible, and Cal's poems turned out not to be Longfellow's.

When he was first getting at these new poems down in the Barn, and we were talking about their metrics, Cal astounded me by saying that he'd heard X give an *Advocate* reading in Cambridge, and that "I knew if he could change, so could I." Cal's new measures are demonstrably looser, the language is less dense, the resonances are buried, true; but the poet of these poems and of *Lord Weary's* is much the same poet, onto a new stage. It is not that Cal has changed, or that except for his effect on poets he has much changed the world. But the Boston Cal came from, which is still much the world of this small peninsula, *is* changing, and that is a truth the town wants nobody to remind it of. Least of all somebody "from away," somebody who seems to be "famous."

I thought that the squalls about *Life Studies* in general, and "Skunk Hour" in particular, had blown out of this harbor a couple of seasons ago. But tonight, two years after the book, I've been drying family laundry in one of the two driers in The Village Laundromat. In through thick fog, to use the other drier, comes a vacationing schoolteacher from Bangor, a woman I grew up with. After we mention the weather, the condition of the driers, and make other small change, she asks if she can ask me something. I nod.

"You write poetry sometimes, don't you?"

I nod.

"Will you tell me *how* a poet like Mr. Lowell can be so famous when he can't even get Jimmy Sawyer on the right island?"

For a moment I don't figure her sense of Cal's leeway, and say so.

"Well, you know that poem about the skunks, the one about him taking his car up into the cemetery?"

I do.

"Well! He says in that one that our selectman works for a woman on Nautilus Island, a woman whose son is a bishop. . . ."

I begin, even in the laundromat, to see.

". . . and everybody knows that that woman on Nautilus never had children, and that Jimmy Sawyer keeps the farm for Miss Harris over on *Hol*brook Island! Now you tell me, how can a poet like that get so famous?"

I cannot tell her. I try, but I do not do well at it. Not while I'm folding hot laundry, not here on the stained old table where she is sitting as we talk. Cal has never been near the laundromat; she has never been near "Notes Toward a Supreme Fiction." Not Stevens'. Not, more specifically, Cal's.

12

In the house on the Common, between the kitchen and the summerroom, there is a small room which must always have been what it still is: part passageway, part storeroom, part woodshed. While Harriet was still being formula fed, it was through this dark passage that the sure smell of burning rubber once drifted out to the adult diners. And back through that passage Cal rushed to fling the smoking sterilizer off the stove and into the sink. For weeks the event became Cal's favorite story, mostly because of the title he gave it: "The Night of the Burning Nipples."

To help care for Harriet, early, Cal and Elizabeth brought with them to Maine a woman from Madrid whose English is still as nonexistent as her sense of service is fastidious. She turns down beds to perfection (an annoyance to Elizabeth, a delight to Cal), she cooks fine paella, she cares for Harriet with large fondness. Now that Harriet is no longer infant but fully little girl, the room between the kitchen and barn has become her special province. She retreats to it after being dutifully presented to guests about to dine; it is her halfway place between her parents' voices around the fireplace and Nicole's Spanish in the kitchen. Harriet, now, is at an all-but-invisible age: pudgy, melancholy-shy with everybody except her friend Johanna or the three adults of this house. She and Robin, our youngest daughter, born the same year, have since babyhood hated each other with the natural desperation of children whose various parents are affectionate friends. Except when Harriet is part of a picnic, we most often see her here: darkly near one or another doorjamb between the kitchen and where adults drink and eat.

Now, as it must have been a hundred years ago, this transitional room partially belongs to the small animals that belong to a child's own growing. This year they are guinea-pigs, long-haired guinea-pigs. Their breed doesn't much matter; they are live, furry, small, and entirely Harriet's own. Or Harriet's and Cal's.

Bringing ice out from the kitchen, Cal stops in the warm gloom of the unpainted passageway, puts the ice-bucket down on the plank floor, and scootches to the fruit-crate level inhabited by Harriet's pets. As Harriet tends them, Cal tends her. All this is all but wordless, as basic as pats and murmurs. Nothing more. Nothing else. Nothing less.

Whatever gets understood here must be what Cal's mother maybe got spoken to him, in some more formal hallway in his own South Shore summers. Unlike anybody else though Cal now is, he must once have been as small, as needful, and as largely adoring, as this half-hidden Harriet. Under the one dull lightbulb hung in the passage he hugs her to his shoulder with total gentleness. Then, with no perceptible transition, he picks up the ice-bucket, and lugs his whole grizzly-bear frame back over the transom into the adult barn.

13

Weir Cove, on Cape Rosier, is about six miles by boat, about twenty-six by car. Once we get there, complete with children, for our here-or-there every-year-or-so picnic with assorted Hoffmans and Eberharts, one feature is inevitable: Dick's taking everybody out around Spectacle Island in his newest prize: a thirty-year-old somewhat Gothic power yacht named the *Reve*. Given the poet each has become, that Dick was Cal's teacher at St. Mark's seems entirely unlikely; unlikely, that is, until both of them get together on the *Reve*. Once, with the two highest landmarks on the East Coast clearly in sight, they talked poetry until the boat was 180 degrees off course in the middle of Blue Hill Bay. Dick has a poem about it; Cal tells it as a suppertable story. If they commonly lack concentration on landmarks like Cadillac Mountain, buoys, and headings, at least they have a common compass in Cambridge: Cal, with some envy and certain delight, sees the *Reve* as "Dick's floating Memorial Hall."

Boats are rarely on Cal's mind; poems almost always are. Today, getting out of their Ford wagon at Weir Cove with his crew, as we pull up with our daughters in ours, Cal wants a moment before we walk down to the Cape Rosier poets and the *Reve*. He tugs me aside, then declaims in his high reading voice the eight lines that will be the third or fourth strophe of "Fourth of July in Maine."

He tells me where the strophe will fit: in the gap I felt this

morning when we were down at the Barn, trading poems. I
remember questioning the early pace of the poem, but I can't
recall how the parts go. I stall: I ask when he got these lines
written.

Cal's head tips sideways with a proudly shy grin: "Driving
over in the car."

14

This morning at his seaside Barn, lying on his cot in the midst
of piles of mail and unopened books, Cal is reading new
Roethke, marking the margins of passages he particularly
likes. He reads me a longish section of a long poem, appar-
ently changes his mind about it in mid-reading, and says it
feels slack when you think of the Whitman it comes from.
Then—his hand angled back from the wrist over the edge of
his cot—he literally pushes the contrast away to the floor. "But
Ted's just *aw*fully good at things like this. . . ." He turns back
to a page he has earlier pencilled, and reads again. "*No*body
can do that better."

In spite of the accelerated pace of his writing (or perhaps
because of it), nobody knows better than Cal the difficulty of
drafting, shaping, intensifying, and—as he says—"tinkering
with" a poem. Roethke, Jarrell, Schwartz, seem to be the poets
he most suffers for. Or with. Long friends, long on pain.
Competitive as Cal can be in semifinal conversation, his gener-
osity to poets he values is without competitive edge. Several
springs ago, when Roethke was reading around Boston, Cal
gathered every known poet east of Amherst for an evening
party on Marlborough Street: that they might meet Ted, that
Ted might meet them. When Cal asked Ted to read, Ted said
he would if Cal would; Cal said he'd be glad to if I. A. Rich-
ards would. When Mr. Richards agreed, if there was a copy of
his new book in the house, it occurred to Cal that he could
invite everybody to read. And up and down he climbed, to
high bookshelves and low, until he'd found a book by every
poet present. And we all read, one poem or two, deferring to

Ted and Cal as Cal deferred to Mr. Richards. Ted had upstage center, deferred to nobody, and revelled in it. Cal let him, happily.

Last year Cal phoned me from New York about the possibility of a Syracuse job for Delmore. And we took him. Cal knew how difficult Delmore was, and was going to be, and said so; but he primarily spoke Delmore's virtues, longstanding and residual. Given the number of people who had given up on Delmore, Cal's concern seems all the more typical: Cal stood by him not because he was last in line but because their friendship was in some way beyond dissolution. The old way. Remembering. Knowing how the world hurts.

It seems to me that caring for poets is, in Cal, based on root fact: having to write poems is one of the terrifying, if sometimes redemptive, joys. Yet Cal keeps at his writing (or his reading-toward-writing) on an almost invariable schedule. And his concentration is such that even being interrupted does not phase him: not if the interruption owes to distress or to poems. I've come to the Barn, unannounced, on both counts; today, our individual and family routines being so different that we haven't in weeks seen each other for real talk, we've prearranged to share sandwiches. I bring a couple of beers.

After Cal's reading Roethke, he remembers things he likes about David Wagoner, and then moves off the cot to the big door overlooking the tide. We sit there, taking our nooning, and talking about nothing but poems. Not his, though his hunt-and-peck drafts are strewn on the floor as they are strewn with inked-in corrections and Cal's misspellings. Not my poems. Today, almost everybody else's between Northumberland and Alaska: H.D. to John Haines. But below our talk, and surfacing constantly in what Cal says, are touchstones from all levels of history. Poems, painters, military tactics, Czarist politics. Even on the new sill of the sagging Barn, sitting in the midst of high noon, Cal is like an archeologist at a dig-site; there are ages and ages under him. I think as I listen how incredibly much Cal knows.

No. I correct myself as I keep listening: I don't know anybody who has felt as much who has thought as deeply.

From the first, Cal has needed people to talk to; I think he imported conversation the very summer he himself was first visiting. And then next year Cal got the Dupees to rent the Brickyard House when he and Elizabeth moved to the house on the Common. The list of people who came visiting at Cal's behest, during these summers, can only sound like a guest-list out of *Gatsby:* Bill Meredith for a day or a week at a time, Bill and Dido Merwin most of one summer. Bill Alfred, quickly in and out from Cambridge, alone; and down from Cambridge, too, Peter and Esther Brooks, and the Bob Gardners—usually en route to Roque Island. Allen Tate, solo; Rollie McKenna, with her Nikons; Fred Morgan, over from Blue Hill; and Andy and Pat Wanning, too, as part of a plank-busting dance in the summerroom. Sometimes Blair Clark, or Bob Silvers, overnight; and Sidney Nolan from Australia; and Elizabeth Bishop, for the best of a week in the Brickyard. And Lord Gowrie, Cal's Harvard student, with the first and only mini-skirted Lady ever observed in these New England parts.

People come to talk with Cal, to listen to how his brilliance works. What's remarkable is how steadily, even with visitors, Cal keeps to his writing routine. Almost daily, Cal's day moves from the old isolation of poems to the strong refreshment of people. Breakfast, postoffice, Barn; work and lunch there until it is time for tennis and people again. People come to talk with Cal; they also come to share Elizabeth's own brilliance, to share her table, to be part of her house. And part of the idea of summer. Almost the only exception to Cal's working schedule is dictated by that alchemy of people and weather which turns a day into a picnic.

We used to go to Ram Island, mostly by way of a couple of outboard-powered rowboats, and by ferrying people on our small sloop. This year, perhaps because the picnics have been considerably enlarged by the arrival of Mary McCarthy and

Jim West, and their household, from Paris, we've gone more to Smith's Mill—a millrace cove with a clamshell beach that lies three miles across the harbor from Cal's Barn.

Over breakfast, the weather comes clear. Mary and Elizabeth, by phone, start collecting people and salads; and, beyond outboard and sail power, a lobsterboat hired from Eaton's Wharf. We all gather there at eleven, and begin to meet each other's visitors. By the time we're all ashore again at Smith's Mill, dinghy-load after dinghy-load, I figure that this has become a picnic to end all picnics. Years ago, I came here with an aged aunt, or boys my own age, to eat jelly sandwiches and dig for arrowheads in the shellheap bank above the shell beach. Today there are over twenty people picnicking by the millrace. To name them, to say the languages being spoken in this mostly lonely cove, is to suggest how much of the world, and what parts of it, have gravitated here—primarily because of Cal.

Harris and Mary Thomas, from Exeter, are talking in French about their memory of Rennes with the newest addition to our crew: an AFS student just arrived from Brittany. Priscilla Barnum is with Margaret and Elizabeth, who trade Georgia talk for Kentucky talk between tending fire and attending to daughters. Margot, our seventeen-year-old Bikini, is putting her highschool Russian to test, listening to Olga Carlisle explaining some nuances of Pasternak's to Cal. As I take some photographs of all this, I have just had it explained to me, by a Classics professor from Cincinnati, that *xai ov,* the name of our dinghy, is badly spelled Greek. Henry Carlisle is talking American English to Sonia Orwell, whose English is British; Ted Draper and James West have given up on Sonia's conversation and have turned to their mutual interest in Poland. Jim, in Polish, asks something of Maria, whom he and Mary have imported from their Paris apartment to serve their establishment here. Native Pole though she is, Maria answers in French; she is helping Jim's sons, Johnny and Danny, dig for flints on the bank above us. Robin and Harriet are huddled in towels on opposite sides of the fire after a quick duck into the local edge of the Labrador current. Carol, our almost-sixteen, has stayed in longer than anybody except Mary

McCarthy—who since coming to Castine has become, by general acclaim, the Champion Stayer-In of All Time. As Mary and Carol stroke slowly toward the shore, Margot comes up to me in full amazement, and speaks (though she does not know it) in that same daughterly voice Thomas Wolfe once heard at his editor's breakfast table:

"*Daaa*ddy, do you know how many languages people are talking here?"

I assent to her amazement.

"You know," she says, "if some Mohawks, or Penobscots, or whoever they'd be, crawled out of that shellheap, *some*body here could probably talk *Indi*an to them. . . ."

Who, for instance?

Her eyes slide down the shell beach toward Cal in his L. L. Bean red shirt, his hands gesticulating wildly. "Well," she hesitates, "*prob*ably Mr. Lowell."

17

Cruising sailors often think of this as a good fogport, and we're fairly used to having old friends descend on us by boat in foul weather. But this August morning, in ample sun, we got a phonecall from an acquaintance on North Haven, asking if we could tonight take care of the friends who are chartering his boat. My father is visiting, Robin's in bed with the flu on this ninth birthday of hers; I was much relieved to find that Margaret and I were only being asked to locate rooms ashore for the charter party and, if possible, to meet them at the wharf when they made port. Then I got told who the charterers were, and how many; they took all the available rooms in the town's one inn.

I'm not used to Kennedys, even junior senators from Massachusetts, much less a whole Washington caucus of Kennedy friends. But they seemed pleased to be met at the wharf when they sailed in casually late; they were grateful for our having found rooms for them; and, yes, they'd love the ten minute tour of the town on the way to their inn. Places where history and revolution happened: the promontory where the French first landed thirteen years before Plymouth, the British fort that frightened Saltonstall into losing his fleet, the Paul Revere bell in the Unitarian Church—all these interest them. Turning, by the church, I point out the house that quartered British officers in 1812; and here, on the opposite corner of the Common, the house where the poet Robert Lowell lives. They might know that just this June, as an act of protest against our involvement in Vietnam, he refused President Johnson's invitation to the White House. They do know. Could they meet him? I offer our Shed and drinks if that wouldn't interfere with their plans. They have no plans, beyond showers immediately and supper much later.

Elizabeth said she wouldn't come, thank you. "I've seen all I want to of those jet-set Kennedy women in their tight pants." Cal was amused, curious, pleased.

In due time everybody arrives at the summer livingroom at the ell-end of our house. Mieke Tunney, and John Culver's wife, and Joan, and Marième and Paul Rugo, seem to have read Cal; John Tunney, and Culver, and Ted Kennedy want to hear from Cal why he turned down the president. They do hear.

Talk gathers momentum though the drinking is slow. I am only on the edge of it, moving around to pass drinks and cheese; going to and from the kitchen. By the sink, Margaret and I exchange impressions; beyond liking Joan immediately, we find we're similarly astonished: these are the people who are running the country, and "they're all younger than we are."

But age is not why they defer to Cal. And as I tend the logs my father has lit in the big stone fireplace, I realize that what started as a casual symposium has mostly turned into a dialogue. Cal is at the fireplace end of the couch, Marième Rugo and Mieke Tunney beside him, across from the big window looking out into fields. The others are variously spread round the room: in wicker chairs, on the bookcase under the window, on the floor by the fire. Just across a low bench from Cal is Ted, sitting in a ladderback chair, leaning forward as far as his backbrace will allow. And he is conducting what has become a kind of subcommittee hearing, question after question being put to the expert witness.

Cal's grasp of politics is new to me, or newly marvellous. Out of nowhere, making analogues from his trip to Brazil, he begins naming South American names, and coming up with figures on income and distribution—figures which sound more like a Kennedy than a Cal. But the hands are Cal's, intensely moving, and so is the voice: a Beacon Hill nasality, varying always in pitch no matter how low the volume. As I go for drinks I catch only snatches:

"I didn't want to lend even tacit approval to what he's begun to do to us."

"*I* don't know what to do about it, Senator; that's up to you." His hand includes Iowa and California. "What I do know is that what we're doing in Vietnam is only more terrible, and more visible, than what we're probably doing in Chile. Or what we've already done in Santo Domingo."

"You know more about power than I do. All I could do was do what I did. I was wrong at first, about wanting to go. It's awkward; it's painful, even, having to refuse a president. He's been good on domestic issues. But abroad we've got to stop him from using power as if it were his rather than ours. It'll take a lot of democracy to stop that."

Ted's voice now: more questions. His respect for Cal is obviously considerable; his courtesy is total. It occurs to me that Kennedy Boston is astounded to find patrician Boston so passionately informed.

". . . I'm conscience bound." Cal stops, then starts again: "We're not only corrupting them, we're corrupting ourselves in the process."

I catch this just coming back into the Shed. The fire has burned low, but none of us seems to have wanted to turn on any lights. In the heavy dusk, the voice at the center of the room is, hauntingly, the voice of an assassinated president.

Ted stops. Then everything quiets.

Cal has said his say.

They came late, and have stayed long. It is only mid-August; but now that everybody is leaving and saying thanks, we are each noticing and saying all at once the same thing: how quickly the dark has come down.

Seascape

George and Mary Oppen in Maine

An afternoon linesquall darkening a Maine harbor. A small sailboat, sails furled against the squall; two figures in foul-weather gear crouched against the sudden rain as their boat slides by the town wharf on the hard run of the incoming tide. The man stands up, intending to anchor, and tosses over a perfectly useless grappling hook. The harbor's too deep, the tide's too strong. As he retrieves his makeshift anchor the boat momentarily disappears in a new rainsquall, then reappears further up-harbor, among the moored fishboats and yachts.

Whoever they are, they're drenched strangers. I row out toward them, point to a mooring they can use, and retreat to the wharf. Waiting for our family dog to come back from ranging the shore as I rowed, I watch the boatpeople rig a tent over their boom and, miraculously, produce from their sixteen-foot sailboat a maybe seven-foot kayak, bright orange, which the woman—I can now see her—must have been inflating under the boomtent. Carefully, as the rain lets up but the tide still runs hard, they ease themselves into the orange toy and paddle with no small skill toward the wharf. I go down the gangway to help them land.

They smile, wet, and say thanks for the mooring. The woman debarks by sliding herself up onto the float, then the man follows while I hold the piece of clothesline they use as a painter. As the woman stands, my big dog, enthusiastically rearrived from his own adventures, noses the woman some-

From *Ironwood* 26, vol. 13, no. 2, (Fall 1985).

what indelicately. She's not in the least flustered. I am. "Pip," I say, "come *here*." The man looks out from under his foul-weather hood: "What did you say his name was?" "Pip," I say, "after *Great Expectations;* one of our daughters named him." The woman smiles: "We once knew a sparrow named Philip."

Wharf-talk has seldom been so literate. I say so. The man asks if I live here, and if I do, do I know Philip Booth. I do and I do and I am. We reach to shake hands. "Oh," he says, apparently reassured but only mildly surprised, "you're who we came to see." He tells me he is George Oppen, and introduces Mary. I'm entirely surprised and immensely pleased. I've read him, of course; it's wonderful that he's read me. The three of us secure the kayak and walk up the hill through the village to the house that was my grandmother's. I introduce Margaret, the Oppens choose tea, and we sit long and long around a big fireplace in the old woodshed that is our summer livingroom.

They stayed for supper; then the wind veered and they went back aboard their little boat to sleep under the boom-tent. I rowed out the next morning to offer breakfast and to give them my new book. They'd already eaten but were glad to read. I have a letter speaking George's detailed response to the poems, and then logging their sail back to Little Deer Isle, where they rented a house that summer at the West end of Eggemoggin Reach:

> Read your poems to each other till
> the tide changed . . . .
>
> The tide changed at 2 in the afternoon,
> I think it was. We tacked out to Rosier,
> turned East to Eggemoggin hooked around
> back of Pumpkin without slowing below four
> knots until Mary luffed for the mooring.
> A dream-like sail. Castine was beautiful
> —nearly beyond belief. The visit beautiful . . . .

This was August of '67, before George's Pulitzer, before Mary's now famous autobiography of their marriage, *Meaning A Life*. They came again, after that first linesquall, in many weathers over a good number of summers. Mostly, given their own natures, the nature of their cruising and of the Maine coast, they showed up unpredictably. One spring, from San Francisco, George wrote fair warning: ". . . we may arrive pyrotechnically on the 4th   But we'll arrive doggedly.   with Great Expectations   Which, if you remember, served to introduce us."

The introduction held, whenever they came. Since they had no car to drive across the Deer Isle Bridge to the mainland, and then the twenty-five roundabout miles to our house, they came instead the slower more direct way: some ten sea-miles around the headland of Cape Rosier to the harbor, always in their same small fiberglass Daysailer, nameless, without state numbers, or even the smallest outboard motor. Having given away the notoriously ridiculous Amphicar that they'd bought in the Bahamas and (if I remember his story) finally driven North, George would have nothing that needed to be licensed. So they sailed; they sailed almost every day that sailing was possible. And if the wind died, they either paddled, or drifted with the tide, or anchored in the lee of one of a hundred islands.

Most days they made sail early in the morning, and usually they were safely at anchor in some new cove, or returned to their own mooring in the gut between Pumpkin Island and Little Deer, before the weight of the afternoon wind was too much for their little centerboarder. They knew how rough the prevailing sou'westerlies could be, especially on an ebb tide. They had a good sense of such local knowledge, but were happily oblivious to fine-tuning their rigging or fitting out their boat in other than improvised ways. Given the slightest breath of dawn air, they hoisted their main and Mary's homemade genoa jib, and tacked among the islands, or ran downwind between them, with small supplies aboard and often—as befits true cruising—with no particular destination in mind. They were pragmatic but adventuresome: save for the then dying breed of native women who—from the early years of the century—remembered their husbands or fathers rowing them between outer islands or in to the mainland, probably nobody on the coast in those Oppen summers knew so many small islands so well. Nobody sailed so often, or so far, in so small a boat.

We live on a peninsula, not an island, but there were days when Mary and George were glad to be on the mainland and to find us home. Once, when the wind backed into the East after a morning's fairweather sail, backed and held there, with nothing but drizzle to ease the fog, they accepted our guest-room for several nights. Margaret cooked, Mary worked on the community quilt that was being made by relatives and village friends for our eldest daughter's wedding, George mostly read boatbooks and nautical lore in front of the fire. We drove inland one morning to buy plants and visit a salmon hatchery; I took George to spend a late afternoon with Cal Lowell, a meeting about which each was slightly uneasy until they forgot poetry and talked on more common ground: family histories and politics. George always had wonderful tales to tell, of his early writing days, of his and Mary's part in the Utica milk strike. He and Mary were easy guests: Mary generously self-sufficient, George happily sheltered by her very presence, by the age of our house, and the fog-dispersing warmth of the fire. That was how and where we most saw them, aside from a memorable supper at Jane Cooper's when she was their Deer Isle neighbor, or now and again (while we still had a boat) as we ourselves cruised near Deer Isle, and chanced or planned to meet them in the sheltered bay inside islands named Butter, Hog, Great Spruce Head, and Pond, a bay in which even the small nubs of grass or ledge have names that appealed to George as much as they always have to me: Two Bush, Fiddlehead, or Dog.

After George and Mary moved further offshore to their Eagle Island habitat we saw less and less of them, at least to the extent that Eagle itself may have partially substituted for their wishing to cruise, and insofar as they the more chose to be isolated. But in whatever summers we best knew them, George and Mary were always—in ways native Maine has always valued—remarkably "the same." He a small hawk of a man, beaked, handsome in profile and knowing it, his talk quietly acute; she more conversational, a woman strongly beautiful, knowing herself well; the both of them strong in spirit, having created a world-within-world for themselves, and being deeply joyed by what they had found and made.

By August '73, after their trip abroad, much as George said that they'd "had a very good time," he also wrote that he was "Exhausted, confused beyond hope." And he wrote that he wanted more than ever now (playing off a poem of mine) "to know, in truth what harbor we are in." There was some inkling of this three years before, when he wrote "We've been doing odd things—the 'world' of poetry: too much for our sense of who we are and who and whatever we are not—Little stability gained in being 62: I'm afraid that's bad news." Margaret and I sensed in this no bad news at all; we were only in our mid-forties, grandparents already, but too young still to know any of the sadnesses of aging. George and Mary seemed immeasurably without age; we much envied their ability "to live" (as I now remember one of Stevens' *Adagia* says) "in the world but outside of existing conceptions of it." What Stevens enclosed in that yearning adage, and closed off in himself, George's poems often say, even as he and Mary sailed such saying, and openly lived it.

They sailed as they lived: pragmatically. When the wind was wrong for a Pond Island picnic they headed elsewhere. If they could not head for Maine in '73, they accepted as given their yearning to be there. From Polk Street in March:

> we think of you and of Maine with longing.
> And yet we decided not to go to Maine this year
> Perhaps we value the longing—those silver
> waters of Castine harbor and those crazy line-
> squalls shine in our heads-----
>
>   we'll let 'em shine
> *there* one summer
>
>   this meaning of Maine to us!
> Childhood, manhood, womanhood—none of us
> will ever say it adequately. But we know about
> it. We know.
>
> (manhood, womanhood, history and the sea and the
> harbors—we can say it easily enough to
> *each other*—!

Each other, yes: Mary to George, George to Mary, and the both of them as Margaret and I, too, tried to say; and as once, in sheer joy of place and weather and being, the four of us at the crossroads bottom of Main Street suddenly stopped walking and had a fourfold hug. "*Un embrazo*," George called it.

George's poems profoundly say to *each other* (within themselves and beyond) how deeply he saw and felt the specific gravity of the coast in those summers when most of it was still comparatively native. Now there's a rash of tourists, an intrusion of strangers, that plagues what was lovely. George and Mary were other than native, but never strangers, not least as they carefully isolated themselves from the exponential changes that now parody the coast's essential character. Aboard what George once called "our hilarious little piece of plastic," they sailed to, and lived within, the very heart of nativeness. They talked and talked to the true natives, and they listened and listened. George knew himself well when he wrote in *Primitive*

> . . . I am
> of that people the grass
>
> blades touch
> and touch in their small
>
> distances the poem
> begins

Sailing their small boat, George and Mary tuned their lives to the "small / distances" that are a measure, in effect a scale, of the intricate composition of Penobscot Bay. George's poems inherently interrelate, even as the islands do in that complex archipelago. Both Oppen poems and Oppen sailing risk heavily tidal deeps, often in search of darkly brilliant harbors where one may be temporarily secure. However numerous the islands, their population is sparse, and the people who natively inhabit those islands must be as adept year-round as George and Mary were in their summers of sailing. I take entirely out of context a few words from Michael Heller's fine new primer on the Objectivists, a book that sharply focuses on

George's theories and George's practice; I find myself realizing that George and Mary sailed in just such ways as Heller argues that the Objectivists wrote: "not out of a . . . sense of mastery of experience, a kind . . . of arrogance, but . . . a show of vulnerability."

Yes, vulnerability. The openness of an open boat in all weathers in an intricate bay of islands. Islanders at heart, as sparsely equipped as some of George's most passionate poems, George and Mary were remarkably like the couple they "Met by chance / On Swan's Island," the woman about whom George speaks in "Ballad:"

> She took it that we came—
> I don't know what to say, she said—
>
> Not for anything we did, she said,
> Mildly, 'from God.' She said
>
> What I like more than anything
> Is to visit other islands . . .

The last time Mary and George sailed into our harbor was in July of '75. They came again on the tide, this time after the wind had calmed; we had already eaten supper when they phoned from Eaton's Wharf. We went down to hear about their trip to Israel, sharing dessert at one of the then new restaurants. They were tired, the trip and their sail up the Bay had both been difficult. We all went to bed early. But even as I was up by six the next morning, there was already on our kitchen table a pencilled note in George's hand. It seems, in retrospect, a foreknown elegy for all their summers on the Maine coast:

> We've spent here some
> of the loveliest days of
> our lives
>
> and now there's a
> lovely wind,—
> love to you all
> G&M

Robert Frost's Prime Directive

"Directive" reads to me like the height of Frost's poetry, the poem he climbed toward for perhaps forty years. Imagery and tone both tell that he's taken this road before: until its last six lines, there's only one image in "Directive" that doesn't appear in, or bear on, some earlier Frost poem. The "children's house" is new; but the apple trees, small animals, and outcrop rock of "Directive" are vintage Frost, here distilled to their metaphorical essence. As his didactic title implies, Frost is familiar with what he's up to. But only here does he newly play guide to his own metaphors and, climbing back to his poetry's wellspring, openly bid a reader to drink at their height.

"Directive" doesn't demand more knowledge of Frost than itself. But the poem gains stature if read as climaxing both the high inclination of, say, "Birches," and the dark temptations of "Stopping by Woods." "Directive" both walks *in* toward self-exploration and, all but simultaneously, works itself *up* toward a theologically marginal grace. The poem is simple to get into. But to be worthy of its final ascent a reader must, by Frost's own example, learn to read the nature with which this poem surrounds him. Earlier Frost poems can teach a reader what to make of deceptively simple natural images, but "Directive" must first be read by submitting to its insistence on "getting lost." Finding-in-losing is the poem's crucial paradox, and unless a reader has been scared by his own desert places he may not be "lost enough" to be guided by Frost through this high-country quest. As it tests a reader's earned humanity, not just his book-learning, "Directive" is in its own way a "serial ordeal"; it can't be read, and wasn't written, as a young man's poem. I remember my own undergraduate distrust of its tones, as Sidney Cox first taught me Frost in that year when it climaxed *Steeple Bush*. I hadn't yet earned reading it. I still perhaps haven't. But now, at least, I know from the mountain poem in *North of Boston,* from the title poem of *West-Running Brook* (and the lesser piece in that book that involves "a broken drinking glass" beside a mountain spring), how much of Frost's writing life was committed to the poem that "Directive" would become. As I've grown older, it seems to me that one of the measures of "Directive" is how greatly Frost tried to make it come whole, how long it took him to discover the cumulative import of images he had always known.

"Directive" doesn't invite us to guess what human ordeals finally drove Frost to write it. Though his biography is full of serial possibilities, the poem asks only that we submit to discovering ourselves in its sense of our common experience. Against this world's temptations to seize the day, "Directive" bids us "back out of all this now too much for us." But Frost's strong stresses, roughened across that great iambic line, admit of no defeat. Precisely because he long knew that "the present / Is . . . / Too present to imagine," Frost begins "Directive" with his familiar gambit of a strategic retreat. As if with Thoreau, John Muir, John the Baptist, or whatever guide has grown wise through days and nights in the wilderness, "Directive" shares with us the possibility of a long perspective on our own emotional history.

Perspective is what the first thirty-five lines of the poem are about, and Frost—in them—is up to his old delight of preparing us for wisdom. There's more ice than fire in these early images of extinction; they notably begin with that "graveyard marble" which suggests our inability to imagine much beyond death. But after its incantatory devastation of house-farm-town, "Directive" recovers our perspective by lending those close losses the context of geologic history. "Monolithic knees" might seem more native to Easter Island than Vermont; but they, like Panther Mountain's "enormous Glacier," lend scale to our mourning and personify those natural forces in whose universe we stand small. We may not know chapter and verse of this long story, but we begin to read ourselves as being part of its book. By Frost's directive, we find ourselves lost with laboring generations of men, exposed to those forty "eye pairs" which steal our courage from us. Unless we invent our own song in this strange land, as Frost requires, there's nothing "cheering" here. But just when our ordeal seems unbearable, Frost reminds us that beside the upstart trees we are comparatively experienced. By the time we climb line 36, we have, in fact, been initiated into the poem's strange lostness. Just as "two village cultures faded / Into each other," we become one with our guide in having lost the accouterments of our civilization. By his directive at this distance from our daily lives, we are mazed in primitive fears, in a nature we see signs of but can't read, in a history larger than our own.

> And if you're lost enough to find yourself
> By now, pull in your ladder road behind you
> And put a sign up CLOSED to all but me.

"Directive" turns on these lines, not least as they restate Frost's casual introduction of their crucial paradox. From here on in, "Directive" climbs on that strange "ladder road" by which we may find ourselves "at home." Frost's "harness gall" metaphor implies, perhaps, how wearing is the burden of paradox; it surely suggests how bitterly minimal our "destination" will be. But here, at least, lostness gives way to finding, the poem's perspective shortens to focus on those few residual symbols by which our humanity is (if barely) sustained. Frost's lines about the children's playthings are, I think, the most heart-rending in all his poetry. "Make believe" though their house may have been, it is also the house (of the farm and the town) in which we once vested belief. This "house in earnest" is now only a "belilaced cellar hole," as impersonal as a "dent in dough"; its shelter may be lost to us, but we find our hearts still in it. Newly children again, we with Frost "weep for what little things could make them glad."

Yet our tears now are more of empathy than of nostalgia; we weep more in tragedy than in terror. Like figures suddenly legendary, we find ourselves become worthy to drink from a "goblet like the Grail." Broken though that goblet is, by the history we too have been lost in, we learn in drinking from it both where we've been and where we've finally arrived. We learn, in fact, to read "Directive" again, to discover human directions in the natural world through which we've been guided. Until its climactic references to the Grail and to Saint Mark, "Directive" reads like an archeological field trip in Vermont (albeit without much compass). The poem's greatness continues to reside in how painfully native to us its least images seem. But as Frost's reference to Mark challenges our memory of the book in which "Directive" is rooted, the reference further guides us to read Frost's images as he would have them read. Frost long said that his poetry was chiefly metaphor, "talking about one thing in terms of another." Mark (4:11) is even more explicit: "Unto you it is given to know the mystery of the kingdom . . . all these things are done in parables." After a night of dark talk, Mr. Frost once reassured me that verses eleven and twelve were his "Saint Mark gospel." (Whoever doubts Frost's salvational sense of metaphor could do worse than look up 4:12.)

"Directive" is, throughout, more metaphor than parable; Frost talks Christian in often secular terms. But its explicit biblical reference further directs us to the source of its chief thematic paradox (Luke 9:24): "For whosoever will save his life shall lose it: but whosoever will lose his life . . . the same shall save it." Frost's sense of being "saved" is as marginal as subsistence farming in Vermont: to sustain one's values, beyond sure losses, depends on being guided by natural signs. Only after we're lost in reading "Directive," and have thus earned a right to its wisdom, do its signs come metaphorically clear. The "cedar" of "Directive," for instance, is natural to Frost's New England; only in the context of the poem's climax does it seem to have been seeded by the cedars of biblical Lebanon. "Barb and thorn" or "ladder road" are similarly metaphors-in-retrospect; they are images of spring floods and steepness before they imply Gethsemane or Jacob. "Directive" is thick with Frost's delight in providing a context that illuminates simple images as the metaphors he intends them to be. The poem is typically Frost in its clear surfaces and complex depths; it's unusual in specifically initiating a reader to what "the wrong ones can't find."

"Under a spell" of metaphor though its ultimate image is, "Directive" is finally a secular poem rooted in residual Christianity. Its biblical references don't, as they might in Stevens, argue for reformation; they don't, as they might in Eliot, invite us back to a church. They measure, instead, both our distance from full redemption and our imaginative thirst for those wellsprings that revive our spirit. Though "Directive" guides us perilously through humanity's common ordeal, its country is no wasteland, there is no chapel at its height. Frost's goblet is merely *like* the Grail; in drinking from it we are still only "near its source." As with the contrary wave in "West-Running Brook," Frost shapes "Directive" as a "tribute of the current to the source," to the Christian drama in which his metaphors are steeped. But Frost is also asking, as he often does, "what to make of a diminished thing." However diminished its symbols may be, Frost seems to imply, our hearts need not let go the value of Christianity's crucial paradox. Yet to imagine our own ordeals as part of a larger drama is not to cast ourselves as heroes; it is simply to realize our share in the human condition. What is heroic in "Directive" is its quiet acceptance of the role to which experience conditions us. Nothing in "Directive" has guided us to hope (whether for a Grail, Redemption, or hope itself); we began to climb without expectation, and end by quenching the unexpected thirst we've earned in sweating uphill. Reality has been our ordeal, and we drink what the poem finally offers us: clear water from a real spring. We are "beyond confusion" not least in this; we are wholly ourselves both in having wept for the children's playthings and in being gladdened by what we made-believe in drinking from their cup. Our imaginative thirst may only be momentarily satisfied, but the poem fulfills itself with a sacrament which redeems our experience by completing our perspective on it.

I read "Directive" as one of those few rare poems that are,

by Frost's definitive hope, "a momentary stay against confusion." The margin of "a momentary stay" is the saving grace of "Directive" and, greatly, its theme. Whoever demands a more ample margin had better be guided up Billy Graham's public aisle; whoever can exist without metaphor had best forget Frost. But whomever "Directive" privately converts (Frost asks no less) can find his margin roughly extended in that strangely unknown Frost poem, "An Empty Threat":

> Better defeat almost,
> If seen clear,
> Than life's victories of doubt
> That need endless talk talk
> To make them out.

Terribly though doubt assailed him, nowhere in his work is Frost defeated by it. Skeptically as a lot of poems talk, nowhere in them is doubt victorious. Nor is there any poem that argues "almost better defeat," whether seen clear or not. What must be seen clear is the poised sequence of those words I've just disordered. My misquote, "almost better defeat," is narrowly, but wholly and perfectly, different from "better defeat almost." The difference is as great as one man's life might be from another's; the distinction in order is, as Frost would have it, of the order of the distinction between prose and poetry. *Defeat-almost* was the ordeal of Frost's life; it is the narrow victory his major poems dramatize, and the human margin of their greatness. As it climbs to marginal redemption through a myth made local by image, through an ordeal heightened by metaphor, "Directive" is one of the greatest. It stays defeat by bettering being lost.

Frost's Empty Spaces

Littleton, Colorado or Littleton, New Hampshire: there comes a December evening, wherever it is cold, out of which snow begins to fall like the dark itself. For skiers it is all promise: recreation, renewal. For men who have grown to know loneliness, and to feel dread, the season when snow comes down like night is a time which confirms all fear. Frost knew. And Randall Jarrell, who deeply understood that "other Frost" who wrote poems less gentle than "Birches," knew why and how Frost felt as he did: "The younger Frost is surrounded by his characters, living beings he has known or created; the older Frost is alone. But it is this loneliness that is responsible for the cold finality of poems like 'Neither Out Far Nor In Deep' or 'Design'."

Jarrell should have added "Desert Places," which belongs with the two poems he names not only in its emotional temperature but in Frost's half-buried history of himself. "Desert Places," too, was published in 1936 as part of *A Further Range,* at the height of Frost's strengths as a poet. He was already sixty-two, and—as the Thompson biography has long since told—he knew loneliness close to home. *A Further Range* was rather coldly dedicated to Elinor Frost, by way of her initials only, in a dedication which began: "for what it may mean to her that / beyond the White Mountains were the Green. . . ." It's hard to know how to take that dedication; it must have been hard for Elinor. But however green their marriage once was, hers and Frost's, it's coldly clear that "Desert Places" is a White Mountain poem in tone, inclination, and context. It is

From *Gone Into If Not Explained,* edited by Greg Kuzma (Crete, Neb.: Best Cellar Press, 1976), 51–60.

the second poem in that section of *A Further Range* called "Taken Singly," a section which begins with "Lost in Heaven" ("Let's let my heavenly lostness overwhelm me") and ends with "Provide, Provide" ("Better to go down dignified / With boughten friendship at your side / Than none at all . . ."). Even beside the poems which surround it, "Desert Places" is, in its finalities, as singularly overwhelming as any poem Frost ever wrote.

Other poems tell, early and late, how much Frost sensed of finalities "beyond the grave." He could drop "The Trial by Existence" from the Modern Library edition of his poems, but he could not dismiss that trial from his life. Time after time, "He thought he kept the universe alone; / For all the voice in answer he could wake / Was but the mocking echo of his own . . . ;" that echo in whatever form was altogether too often, for Frost, not only "The Most of It," but was "all." Emotionally, literally, and metaphorically, "Desert Places" informs, and is informed by, the remarkable range of Frost poems which make, around it, a jagged horizon.

Within "Desert Places" itself, of course, there is practically no horizon. Save for the few specifics which catch Frost's eye, and the speculations to which those specifics give rise, the poem is mostly monochromatic. Beyond its "blanker whiteness of benighted snow," the poem stretches specifically outward only for a moment of bravado: "They cannot scare me with their empty spaces / Between stars. . . ." But of course there are no stars in the storm; play as it does at the bravado which shapes a great deal of Frost's first book, *A Boy's Will,* that isolate first line of the last stanza of "Desert Places" becomes, in context, quickly ironic. The most of the poem belongs to a less defiant Frost: the Frost who knew as if from the first, almost in spite of himself, that night, dark, seasons of storms and dark woods were not merely "the merest mask of gloom" but did, in fact, stretch "away unto the edge of doom." Those words are not only from Frost's first book but from that book's first poem, "Into My Own." "Desert Places" is far beyond Frost's first self-persuasion that he "will be rather more than less himself for having forsworn the world;" "Desert Places" is in many ways the naturally lonely culmination of poems like "Storm Fear," "The Fear," some of "Snow," "An Old Man's Winter Night," "Fire and Ice," and even the poem which it circumstantially and formally resembles: "Stopping By Woods on a Snowy Evening."

Long before "Desert Places," Frost had already found himself as one "Acquainted With the Night"; by this time in his poetry, the "Snow falling and night falling fast oh fast" in no way tempts him to stop by the field he says he "looked into going past." Everything in those first lines expresses a desire *not* to "look into" this snowstorm. Not any more than a man, out of self-protection, must. The lines themselves move with what might be the inclination of a man hurrying home against a threatening sky; they surely move with the speed of snow and night falling, falling together. But then, as the ground is "almost covered smooth in snow," the poem begins to slow as it takes on weight. Before winter totally sets in, it is not any sign of potential renewal which Frost can find to notice; in this deserted field he can see only "a few weeds and stubble showing last."

"Showing last." The last earthly signs: stubble and weed. The line goes far beyond "the end / Of a love or a season" (as "Reluctance" once said); the finality is self-demonstrated by the order of Frost's periodic sentence. From here on out (quite literally), the poem sees nothing save absence. And from its close-in thought for "All animals . . ." who "are smothered in their lairs," the poem moves typically toward Frost's concern with the cosmos-at-large—not, in this circumstance, toward some starry semblance of order, but to "the empty spaces / Between stars." From that huge sense of absence, the poem and the poet will come back close to "home."

Except for the contrivance of the fourteenth line's rhyme, the end of the poem is too blankly stated, too emotionally conclusive, to admit of much question. Frost closed off the poem tightly, and let it go at that. He wasn't about to say more. Openly existential as the poem generally looks to readers some forty years after Frost wrote it, the Frost who wrote "Desert Places" wasn't trafficking in philosophic abstractions; he was getting down to whatever it was in himself that so seldom dared bare itself. Who knows, finally, what it was?

When the poet finally returns the poem to himself, when he finally admits "I have it in me so much nearer home / To scare myself with my own desert places," I only know that I momentarily forget the poem and think back to how Mr. Frost, already an old man, first gave me a glimpse of his night side.

He was close to seventy-five. I had just started to think about words; there were better than fifty years between us. I'd known Mr. Frost slightly since 1943; my wife and I had seen a fair lot of him in the several winters since our marriage. Mr. Frost and I had talked alone that night at the Hanover Inn until eleven, but when I got up to leave he waved his hand negatively across his chest: "No," he said, "I'll walk you home." I can remember still how that mud-season midnight smelled, I remember the heaved town sidewalks; what we talked about I don't remember at all. I only know that when we got to my corner, more than a half-mile from the inn, I again said good-night.

Mr. Frost shook his head. "I walked you home, now comes your turn. You have to walk me."

It was night, late, dark: the issue was, at heart, although I barely then realized it, how to part and get home through more night, toward whatever sleep would come later.

Back and forth, forth and back. We walked East Wheelock Street four times at least, maybe six. Finally, halfway down my way, it being his turn as guide, Mr. Frost stopped, stood talking, and decided: "Enough for one night." He reached out to shake hands. "You go your way now, I'll go mine."

That was all. I guessed that I'd been initiated. But into what, beyond Mr. Frost's trust, I was far from sure. There were a good number of those nights over the next twelve years: Maine, Bread Loaf, Cambridge. But only when I myself lay sleepless, shaken, and empty in the attic room of another inn, the night before Mr. Frost's funeral, did I realize how often he had walked me (and many others) forth and back to being halfway home. Only then did I realize that just as the public Frost, the platform Frost, rushed talk-between-poems to fill up silence, so the private Frost walked—talking or composing himself—to (literally) pass the night.

The night of "Desert Places," though, is no night to be out;

not even as the first stanza ends with the snow deepening over dead ground. But the second stanza, even as it specifically validates, and leads to, the dreadful abstractions which follow it, is the stanza which says most about Frost's night side. The leap from the last line of the first stanza to the first line of the second is, perhaps, as dramatic a leap as occurs between any two lines in all of Frost's work: from the "few weeds and stubble showing last" he moves to a remarkable line that is all the more remarkable in being Frost's: "The woods around it have it—it is theirs." Of the four substantives in this pivotal line, three are "it." Not only is each "it" totally without antecedent at this stage of the poem, but the "it" is presented as being too dreadful to substantiate further. The woods are said to "have it" as if it were, in fact, a dreadful contagion. And it is. The woods may be "around it" just as woods often surround a field, but this "it" is no mere field, however deserted, however impinged upon by raw nature. The woods are not only "around it," but just as they simultaneously "have it," so also "it is theirs." Theirs in spite of themselves. Theirs beyond choice. To sense what "it" implies, beyond the context of this line, a reader might think back through that dark quality of those other woods which tempted Frost to stop by them; or one might think forward to the "design of darkness to appall," a design which is not only the title of "Design" but its appalling subject and dark theme.

By the time a reader reaches the eighth line of "Desert Places" he may be tempted to feel that the referent for each of the first three uses of "it" is, after all, "loneliness." And so, through lines nine and ten, it partially is. But to talk about "it" simply as "loneliness" would be to move from almost speechless dread of the unidentifiable to an abstract word for one of its elements. "Loneliness" is only one element in the poem; it is not, for instance, what has "smothered" the animals in line six. This is no poem about woodchucks being smugly snug in their burrows; this is a poem in which "All animals" appear to be "smothered" by what totally overwhelms them, and that other animal in the poem: the man-animal, Frost. "Snow falling" is what may literally cover the animals' lairs; but in the coincidence of "night falling" what all-but-smothers Frost's ability to speak is precisely what he manages to speak in line five: the ineffable "it."

Frost breathes in line seven with what at first feels like relief: "I am too absent-spirited to count." But as the next line makes clear, Frost feels himself too "absent-spirited" to *be counted:* "The loneliness includes me unawares." The line is perfectly ambivalent in its energies. And so, suddenly, does the "loneliness" extend beyond merely one man's isolation to imply the very source of loneliness, some source of absence (as if in the empty spaces between stars) that is, itself, so abstractly "absent-spirited" as to include Frost "unawares." Alone of all animals in this self-affrighting poem, Frost seems to own no lair from which he might escape it.

Unlike the people of another short Frost poem, the people who keep long-shore watch over all they cannot comprehend, Frost himself looked both out far and in deep. The dramatic poems are perhaps those that look in most deeply at what he was otherwise most reticent to show: how marriages give and take. Between "in deep" and "out far" in Frost's poetry, there are surprisingly few middle distances. Whenever he found himself in too deep, Frost—like the man in "The Star-Splitter" who burned down his house to buy a telescope to find his place "among the infinities"—kept a lifelong night-watch, hoping to find "something like a star / To stay" his mind on. Running away to Kitty Hawk from Elinor's first refusal of him, or returning there in 1953, Frost looked long and far for evidence of what he talked about as "the descent of the spiritual into the material." There wasn't much evidence of such annunciation in his own family life; there wasn't much that stayed him close to home. He talked tangentially about it, when he could bear to. He walked a lot of it out. And sometimes he wrote it, this poet for whom a poem was, by self-definition, "a momentary stay against confusion." "Desert Places" isn't much of a stay, but nothing could be less confusing than Frost's sense of this whitely deepening dark night. Lonely as Frost is in the poem, and even more lonely as he will be, he is at least able to bare himself to, and to bear, whatever it is that is so "unawares" that it doesn't even account for him, or for his spirit. The poem knows it as Frost knew it. By the end of the poem he can admit to himself "I have it in me. . . ." To scare himself. To write "Desert Places." The poem is not only the poem of the words, but the poem of the empty spaces between them.

Wallace Stevens'
Domination of Black

Except when Stevens invents fancy variations on his basic dialectic, he's a marvel. Given the neatly free-floating qualifier in his prose adage, "In poetry at least the imagination must not detach itself from reality," I'm willing to forgive a lot of what he elsewhere belabors. I like nothing better in Stevens than how his ambivalences balance. I like the Thurber-comedy of "A Rabbit as King of the Ghosts" almost as much as I admire that most demanding of all single-sentence poems, "The Snow Man." I have long fondness for Stevens' ". . . Ordinary Evening . . . ," and for the extraordinary gray day of "No Possum, No Sop, No Taters." Over and over, in Stevens, I am touched by the minimal that refuses to be reductive.

Of all the "balances that happen" in Stevens, whether abundant or bleak, none has moved me longer than "Domination of Black." I woke late to what Frost called the "design of darkness"; I was maybe twenty when "Domination of Black" first appalled me. I've half grown used, now, to such dark as the poem involves, but I've never outgrown being stunned by the questions the poem turns in on itself, combining what he would later call "the philosopher's search // For an interior made exterior / And the poet's search for the same exterior made / Interior. . . ." For years I was stunned into blind misreading: I wanted every aspect of the peacocks, not only "the colors of their tails," to counter the night and its "heavy hemlocks." I wanted the last line of the first strophe, emphatically repeated

From *Field* no. 21, (Fall 1979).

as the last line of the full poem, to begin with "But. . . ." But Stevens, twice, wrote his own clear sentence: "And I remembered the cry of the peacocks."

Since my imagination had so demonstrably detached itself from the reality of the poem, it took some extraordinary actuality to make me understand how deeply Stevens' imagination was dominated by emptiness. Maybe ten years ago, my youngest daughter and I, flashlights in hand, searched into the March woods near our house for the source of a cry-of-distress she was sure she'd heard. I was skeptical until I heard, too, a voice, almost strangulated with fear, crying "Help!" But the sound moved toward us as we moved into the woods, and it turned out to be no more or less than the cry of the apparently lonely peacock just acquired by a doctor who lived down the road. The doctor knew, of course, when we told him how close the peacock's cry came to the cry of a human voice.

Stevens knew, and wrote "And. . . ." He had just written in "Domination . . ." what is, perhaps, his most emotionally revelatory line: "I felt afraid." He wasn't about to say more; he let the peacocks confirm his fear and climax the poem, a poem that is truly "the cry of its occasion, / Part of the *res* itself and not about it." It is the poem I remember now, not the house we used to live in, or the woods my daughter and I tried to search. The bird and the doctor are dead. It is the poem I think of when I see out the window how the planets gather, when I feel in myself the color of the heavy hemlocks.

William Carlos Williams

An Open Thanksgiving

It must have been in the winter of 1948–49 that I first heard Dr. Williams read: to maybe thirty people at the 92d Street Y. Some ten years later I heard him after his stroke read "Of Asphodel . . ." at Wellesley, where the full-house audience gave him long silence before long applause. In the years between I'd listened to his part of Lloyd Frankenberg's remarkable anthology/record, "Pleasure Dome," and as I'd read and reread Williams I began to hear how his poems come off the page.

I've never understood Williams' defense of his "variable foot," but I'm certain I hear the strengths of his sense of measure, whether the line is stepped or not. From the beginning, he tuned his lines to how he kept hearing American speech; whenever I heard him his own voice was harsh, sharply uneven, almost sexual in its energies. Whether his subject is the misery of an Elsie or his own joy in bowing to a young housewife, his total attention to his subject (as if he were listening to one of his patients) genuinely informs the pressure of his lines and the pace at which they let words release their import.

Paterson says how long, and in how many ways, Dr. Williams attended to words, to the American language made up of them. But it's the earlier poems which most openly demonstrate how the words are weighted or lightened by the line,

From *William Carlos Williams: Man and Poet,* edited by Carroll F. Terrell (Orono, Me.: The National Poetry Foundation, 1987), 47–50.

and how the line takes its shape and pace from the nature of the words. A prime example is surely the second stanza of "To a Poor Old Woman," where the poem opens to immediate joy in the various ways the plums "Taste good / to her" and "taste / good to her." Only as he here presents the immediacy of her tasting can the poem finally come down, and around, to the solace given her by the simple fact of "munching a plum on / the street." The doctor's attention is notably on *her* response— on her response as he gives voice to it. No less is true in "To Waken An Old Lady." Different as its jagged measure may be, there is Williams' familiar attention to where the voice is inclined to pressure or release this word or that, and to how such events lighten or weigh the line and so tip the poem's balance. The fulcrum in "To Waken . . ." is, of course, the syntactic interjection of a harshly natural question: "— / But what?" What question can be asked, what prescription given, to waken her? Again the attention is clinically particular yet emphatically human. In finding words for how his subjects fall the poet finds voice for how his own words rise. Just as in the so-called "Red Wheelbarrow," the poem's moves toward resolution depend on the very problem the poem initially poses.

Tactically as well as emotionally, Williams began to write each poem by making a start out of particulars. And those particulars included, however intuitively he came to them, syntax as well as measure. Williams has long since proven to be one of the Old Masters at making a poem new. The primitive syntax of "To a Poor Old Woman" has by now become a modernist cliché; so has such an interjectory question as shapes "To Waken An Old Lady," insofar as such a question makes for immediacy of voice. Williams' sense of measure has for years been measured and remeasured, but practically no critical attention has been paid to Williams' highly individual syntax. I hear the poems' syntax as being as important as their prosody; both tactical factors are primary elements of how openly a Williams poem validates itself.

I don't presume to be able to define the varieties of his syntax; I mean now only to point to it, given the pleasure I take from how strongly it works. Consider, for instance, the interjection "Let us see, let us see!" in "Waiting," a poem in which the first strophe is syntactically commmonplace, but acute in how its lines counteract the plainness of statement. "Let us see, let us see!" looks to be an interjection plain and simple, save only as doubling multiplies it tonally. But given the culminating question of the poem, as these words introduce it, they retroactively seem (beyond mere interjection) to be a petition for insight. Casual as such syntax appears to be, it is part of how the poem opens itself to a variety of emotional possibilities. I marvel at the still greater openness, and emotional complexity, of that remarkably unnoticed poem "A Portrait in Greys," where the misery of the speaker becomes, in the intricate syntax of the whole final sentence, subordinate to his (or, I would guess, *her*) concern for the subject of the portrait: the person whose emotions she cannot fully engage. Again, a series of questions move the poem toward its climax, questions in which the syntactic energy and rhythmic torque are each part of the other:

> Must I be always
> moving counter to you? Is there no place
> where we can be at peace together
> and the motion of our drawing apart
> be altogether taken up?

I marvel and I am, in all senses, moved. What a joy Williams is, even in this poem's intense misery. He realizes it! Always beyond self-pity, he realizes emotion *through* the poem, realizes it and releases it for sharing. Not only is Williams more unself-consciously open to experience than most poets, he opens his poems to every possibility of letting a reader experience them. His poems clearly invite a reader to share. He *wants* to share, to let the poem open our own emotion even as his emotion is given voice in the process of making the poem. Measure and syntax make his voice vitally present on, and beyond, the page; he makes a gift of how the experience gets said. And how broad and deep the experience is. What life there is to the poems! What vital fire in "Portrait of the Author." And not only in such famous field-and-weed poems as "Queen-Ann's-Lace" and "Great Mullen," what marvellous taste (beyond any mere bitterness) in *Sour Grapes*. Who among us has been at once so open and so resilient?

The particulars of measure and syntax inform, literally inform, every Williams poem, yes, from its very beginning. But behind and within such particulars there's a generosity, an essential humanity, that no medical school or poetry workshop can presume to teach. To read Williams closely is to learn useful tactics, of course. But to read him well is most of all to meet in the poems some fine part of one's self, to immediately experience not only one man's life, or one physician's city, but something close to the nature of a place, maybe even a country where democracy might actually be practiced.

Large-scale abstractions weren't Dr. Williams' stock-in-trade; democracy, as such, was seldom his explicit subject. But his concern and his practice were as open as his poems. In his reading at the Y in the late forties, he spoke more than indirectly, and not without harsh humor, of the practice of poetry in this particular country. Dr. Williams was already sixty-five, and still widely unknown. In the awkwardness of the notably small audience, and his own awkward readings from Lorca, Dr. Williams after a while gave himself pause by asking for questions. Someone, without intending irony, asked what he saw as "the function of the poet in America." He drew back, startled, half-embarrassed that he'd seemed to ask for such asking.

Then he said, "Who was it wasn't it Aristophanes who marched naked at the—what, you know—Pan-Athenaic Festival? That was how the old Greeks treated their poets: a poet at the head of the parade." He thought a while, building to a grin, and to what still are, in effect, the energies of his poems: "But the function of a poet in America? Imagine *me,* on the Fourth of July, walking down the Main Street of *Pate*rson in my *jock*strap!"

Prose Notes on Prosody

1) "The prose poem" is, to my ear, a contradiction in terms; no matter how interesting its substance, it comes dull to my ear. Unduly dull, like an Economics text that hasn't yet heard of even prose rhythms. Whatever a poem's "prosodic freedom," its prosody partially depends, by definition, on the fact that the poem is composed of lines. Lines and lines. A line is the poet's springboard: a recurrent chance to balance, spring, clown, play Icarus, to enter the same old pool in a hundred new ways.

2*a*) A line for me is a measure of measure; no matter how variable that measure, it moves the poem as it involves both recurrence and duration. I'm newly most excited by lines that establish, or illuminate, a syntax that's more ambivalent than prose can possibly be.

 b) I dislike the idea of "exploiting" a line-break; my sense is more of making a line-break function in ways that extend beyond the line, or the line-break, itself. This isn't so natively easy as it sounds. Look at the thousands of poems in print that have no ear whatever for such possibility.

3) The old British base, quantitative/qualitative verse, now seems to me, in an Einsteinian multiverse, to have primarily ironic function. The virtues of that irony can be as heroic as Anthony Hecht's *The Hard Hours*. But when it is impossible to measure quality *as well as* quantity beyond any Newtonian standard, I find myself feeling more and more at home in

From *Epoch* 29, no. 2 (Winter 1980).

such uncertain fields as Heisenberg first outlined. These fields are where I live. I need Basie as well as Mozart at various times of various days; I listen to each with separate devotion. But only in the lines of my own poems do I know to make my own music.

4) "Is the line a unit of inspiration" for me? No, except in the most literal sense: until I can *feel* how my first line sounds, I have no idea how the rest of the poem may breathe, or hold its breath, or play or resist what may come to be its fundamental measure of vitality. A line, as such, makes me catch my breath only to the extent that it has an end: a place in the poem to bear down from, to hold back on, to let up with, or shift speed across.

5) I think my mixed metaphors say something of how multiple my concerns are: "the line" doesn't so much "accommodate them" as catalyze them.

6a) Thirty years ago, when I was just beginning to write, I could hear in myself the plain flatness of the opening lines of "Directive," and I could feel in myself the tug when Wilbur's "He Was" moves into its line, and I was knocked over (and over) by how Hopkins made his lines spring. I'm still moved by all these ways of moving a reader into a poem. But after I'd seen and heard my own first book, I wanted lines that were differently stressed, that were closer to my own life-rhythms, even to my body-language; I began to experiment with how my lines could work off the beat rather than with it. Williams' poem about Breughel's Kermess excited me; so did some of Olson's ideas about Projective Verse; so did something I now forget in Rosalie Moore's *The Grasshopper's Man.* But it was always how the line contained and/or released its energies that moved me more than the idea of a line as a unit. This is still true in the work of poets who've more recently gotten my ear. Or more than my ear: as my own ways of hearing have changed, I'm more than ever concerned about what I now feel as the torque of a line.

  b) The title poem of my first book, *Letter from a Distant Land,* probably speaks the standard my ear was then tuned to. A number of the short-lined poems in *The Islanders,* most notably "Was a Man," still sound my sense of moving into the offbeat—I hear this as analogous to a drummer adding a hi-hat to the snare and bass he's already working. I think my ear got more subtle as my work grew, but my concern for a line, as such, didn't much change until it assuredly opened in "Lives," the closing poem of *Available Light.* My new book goes from there, I believe; I have to believe. But the more I think about these questions, the more certain I am that what I've said is only half true. The other half, the truth I don't know to say, is the music my lines chiefly come from and mean to inform.

A Distinctive Voice

I don't think about "voice" as such; I talk aloud to myself when I write, but I mostly listen for rhythms and how they get shaped and paced by internal patterns of sound. I suppose I have a New England voice, in some larger sense: direct, slightly flat, perhaps dry. My sense of a subject and my attitude as I'm writing makes, I hope, for various voices in various poems; but within that flexibility I want tones constant to my way of seeing and saying: a kind of understatement that's not (however wry) without some sense of humor.

I'm tired of irony; it's been taught to death. What I want to hear in a poem is not a teacher's voice talking (my own included); I'm after something closer to conversational metaphors, to how stories shape themselves into self-resolution through casual re-telling. I revise and revise, line by line, but not until I've first found the rhythms and tones that feel native to the poem that the poem is trying to become. I write from the beginning, as well as I word-by-word can, trying to discover how the experience of the poem may, in the end, resolve.

The world's not apt to be resolved by a poem, but a poem can make the world's landscape more humanly bearable, maybe more bearably human. Whether that impulse is what charges "a poet's voice," this year or any year, I don't presume to guess. I'm certain, though, that we don't need another *Waste Land* to tell us where we live. Our problem is less to define the world's complexity than it is to discover, within that complexity, some

From *The Distinctive Voice: Twentieth Century American Poetry*, edited by William J. Martz (Glenview, Ill.: Scott, Foresman, 1966).

marginal way of sustaining how we relate to it. A poem does nothing for me if it doesn't stretch to do that. The voice of any good poem, whatever wilderness it cries from, cries less than it says "Hello, out there!" I forget the name of the one-act play that Saroyan built from that line, but the line is one act of a poem. A good poem greets the world; it welcomes the sharing a listening reader completes. The world's always out there, often mute but seldom inglorious: a poem or a person waiting for words.

But maybe my hope for a poem's too ideal. I know that I also write to make sense of my own experience. There are days when I'm short of courage when I selfishly write to hear my own voice: when I need to speak back some old "hello" to myself.

Eaton's Boatyard

To make do, making a living:
                              to throw away nothing,
practically nothing, nothing that may
come in handy;
                    within an inertia of caked paintcans,
frozen C-clamps, blown strips of tarp, and
pulling-boat molds,
                         to be able to find,
for whatever it's worth,
                              what has to be there:
the requisite tool
                    in this culch there's no end to:
the drawshave buried in potwarp,
chain, and manila jibsheets
                              or, under the bench,
the piece that already may fit
                                   the idea it begins
to shape up:
                 not to be put off by split rudders,
stripped outboards, half
a gasket, and nailslick garboards:
                                      to forget for good
all the old year's losses,
                              save for
what needs be retrieved:
                              a life given to
how today feels:
                    to make of what's here
what has to be made
to make do.

The Creative Process
INTERVIEWED BY ALBERTA T. TURNER

1. The poem starts to make a statement about what is needed "to make do, making a living" in the context of a boatman's life. For more than a page it details the kinds of choices to be made ("to throw away nothing . . . that may come in handy," "to be able to find / . . . what has to be there," "to make of what's here / what has to be made," "To find the piece that already may fit") from a detailed jumble of wornout or random or misfit bits of boat-building stuff. The poem, though it ends with a period, does not put a verb to the long list of infinitive subjects, much as the builder of a boat or a poem or a life never completes the job of choosing and making and remaking with whatever materials happen to be within reach. Was this syntax calculated to make the reader expand the meaning and again expand it in this fashion? Have your readers tended to expand it as far as you want them to? Farther?

No, the syntax was in no way "calculated"; I discovered in the process of writing, revision after revision, how constantly the implications expanded. And, I would hope, deepened. How deeply a reader cares to look into the poem depends, I guess, on how well my syntax presents my sense of relationships. Early in *Before Sleep,* a poem called "Words for the Room" speaks my inclination toward "infinitives, relative objects." In all possible senses.

2. As a reader who spent many summers of my youth sailing an old gaff-rigged, ex-clam boat off Nova Scotia, I recognize the different kinds of necessity and the condition of many of the objects in "Eaton's Boatyard." Our sails, too, were patched and our ropes much spliced. I don't recognize culch, pulling-boat molds, potwarp, but I do most of the others. Would it make a difference, do you think, to the impact of the poem if I recognized none of them? If the boatyard were an auto repair shop? A gardener's tool shed?

This poem began long before I began to write it. It's a distant relative of a poem of mine called "Cleaning Out the Garage," and an even earlier poem called "Jake's Wharf," a wharf that was, in my boyhood, next door to Eaton's Boatyard. This poem descends more directly from another early poem called "Builder," which is about the grandfather of the boy who gave me one of this poem's prime words. The boy was about thirteen, I was maybe forty, still hanging around the waterfront, when I heard him yell to his father, Alonzo Eaton, "Dad, *when*'re you going to clean up this *christly* culch?" I missed the ultimate word the first time he yelled, but I got him quieted to say it again. And when I got back home to an unabridged dictionary, there it was: a word so old that Cabot or Champlain may have imported it to my home coast, a word I trust is as self-explanatory in the context of the poem as it was when the boy first yelled it.

Culch may be, in the poem, more self-evident than *potwarp* (the kind of rope that attaches a lobsterman's buoy to his trap far below it), or *pulling-boat molds* (the wooden patterns around which old Maine rowboats were built), but I've tried, all through the poem, to build around such terms a sufficient context for whatever reader may share my delight (with Hopkins) in "áll trádes, their gear and tackle and trim."

3. Your book Before Sleep, *in which this poem appears, contains a wide variety of poetic forms, a number of which seem to be selected for the sake of their visual effect. Is this poem's appearance on the page selected for that reason?*

No. Except as white space around dark print is a kind of visual notation even in sheet music, I don't think of my poems as being an eyeful. Not least as I hear line-ends as being variously inflexed, I feel the lineation in *Before Sleep* as being notational: as being one part of indicating hesitancies, holds, surges, in the overall score of the poem. I mean to help attune readers to how the poem wants to be heard.

4. What determined your rhythms and sound repetitions?

My ear. After years of practicing traditional English meters, and then moving to the roughened voice of accentual verse, I've here turned back toward what I early heard in Hopkins and, even earlier, in jazz: the offbeat working against the drumfoot. These influences, in ways I'm not sure I want to understand, work in me now as rhythms of my body language driving the poem to find its own music.

5. If the poem is also a description of how you work at your own craft of poetry, how would you identify the throwing away of "practically nothing," the "culch," the disorder of the shop, the way the piece that already fits "begins to shape up" the idea, the "old year's losses"?

Yes. I think, after the fact, that the poem *is* about the inevitable process of giving one's life, or one's poem, to what comes of feeling down into the materials at hand. Even in the culch of Eaton's Boatyard or the apparent chaos of being alive, nothing is ever lost. The problem of what to make of what's here (where else, after all?) is always, for me, a matter of piecing together what presents itself with "what needs be retrieved" in order to make sense of what's present.

6. What started the poem? What revisions did it go through, in what order, over what period? If you have saved the worksheets, may I see a copy?

I knew for years that there was a poem in Eaton's Boatyard. But only when a friend from (improbably) Paris made me a present of her unread (she said "unreadable") copy of *The Savage Mind* did I find Lévi-Strauss making his own distinction between the bravely planned world of the Engineer and the "devious means" of the person he calls "the *bricoleur*." Once I'd read his marvellous first chapter (and, indeed, found the rest of the book beyond me), I had only to retrieve the word *culch* before I found myself writing the present poem.

The draftsheets are far from me now, in a library. The poem as it has come to be completed has displaced those drafts in my mind. I'd guess that there are twenty to thirty draftsheets (fairly typical for me, given a poem of this length and complexity); my draftsheets are themselves a measure of process, of incrementally imagining "the piece that already may fit / the idea it begins / to shape up," of listening and listening to how words build to normative (and variant) lines, of how lines break to integrate (and vary) triadic forms, of how the pace of the poem is itself a measure of "what has to be made" to do justice to the materials: to bring feeling into such meaning, and meaning into such feeling, as the materials implicitly offer. The poem itself is what I have made "to make do."

Dreamscape

On the steep road
curving to town, up
through the spruce trees
from the filled-in canal,
there have been five houses, always.

But when I sleep
the whole left side of the blacktop
clears itself into good pasture.
There are two old horses,
tethered. And a curving row
of miniature bison, kneeling,

each with his two front hooves
tucked in neatly under the lip
of the asphalt. I am asleep.
I cannot explain it. I do not
want to explain it.

How a Poem Happens
INTERVIEWED BY ALBERTA T. TURNER

1. How did the poem start?

From the beginning. Always from the beginning, trying to recover the original impulse and move the poem with it. Always, back to the beginning, to be moved by the impulse, to make the poem move.

In this particular poem the title begins to tell.

2. What changes did it go through from start to finish?

All possible changes that might, as I sensed and tested them, writing and rewriting, enable the poem to move toward its own conclusions. All changes that might both explore those conclusions and, naturally, light their way.

3. What principles of technique did you consciously use?

None, consciously. No principles as such. A poem consciously principled belongs to a School before it's begun; or ought to be left to poetry workshops: purely an exercise.

Principles inhere: say how a lifetime inhabits earthspace. How a voice gets down on a page is mostly another matter.

A poet in the process of writing need be no more or less aware of "techniques" than a skijumper approaching the lip of a jump. On hills where darkness has closed down early, he has already learned by example, and practiced every possible technique. Readied, he is full of experience and feeling, set to inhabit blank air. What may once have felt mechanical becomes, in process, organic: his form is an event: an act of intensely concentrated motion both grounded in common sense and defying it.

First courage, then skill, then luck. The luck that courage and skill help make. Worrying about a principle as basic as gravity can only bring the poet down hard; tactics become reflex are what accomplish the leap. There's some unspoken poet in every skijumper: who else leans out so far and learns,

77

briefly, even in mid-flight, how to reshape the whole course of his life?

4. Whom do you visualize as the reader?

One person and one person and one person. Never, collectively, "an audience." Never, as I write, editors. Sometimes, on the far margins of my first feeling, this person or that whose art (not necessarily poetry) has lent courage to my own. But I believe the reader I hope for, reading late by simple light, is bound to be out there: one—or one with another. The person will find the poem if the poem finds the person. Writing, writing, I try only to get back, down, and out to what the world of the poem may come to.

The oldest commandment is still first: Honor Thy Subject.

5. Can the poem be paraphrased?

I trust not.
"Dreamscape" is in part about a refusal to paraphrase complex perception, and that part of the poem can probably be "talked about." Around-and-about, which is probably more illuminating than the ways that paraphrase thinks are "direct." Paraphrase, as distinct from close reading, is almost always reductive. A good poem never is: the nature and quality of its concerns are too surely human and too surely eventful. In subtracting the eventfulness, paraphrase discounts humanity.

The recurrences in "Dreamscape" seem to me, long after the fact, to reinforce my emphasis on what may be the poem's pivot-word: "always." Short of the poem itself, what lesser statement might give that word its due, or tell by context its tone?

6. How does this poem differ from earlier poems of yours?

QUALITY. Asked to guess, I wouldn't want to confuse the always singular present with the continually plural past. The poems I've earlier written are already a grove: hardwoods and softwoods, evergreens, and deciduous trees of all sizes. This apparently small poem is more likely to be shaded out by new growth than to thrust up through old. But it might seed some strong new roots. I didn't know when I wrote it. I still wouldn't want to pretend to.

THEME. It would take a reader almost as familiar with my poems as I am, and more objective, to judge the growth of my themes. I rarely look back at my earlier books; when I do, I find myself mostly amazed. I am always more interested in what I am writing than what I have written.

TECHNIQUE. Before I was old enough to be a parent, yet was, I thought that poems like *L, M, O,* were so accomplished that they clearly fulfilled the promise of what a poem could be. Now that I'm old enough to be a grandfather, and am, my belief is in more difficult trusts: the round of enigmas and ambivalences and mysteries that make life the most certain poem of all, the poem I hope my own poems may increasingly honor.

States

Thought it was still New Hampshire,
now it's Vermont. And I have to
keep going. On up the White River valley,
wanting to find the old village inn I want
to turn back to a theatre.
                 I keep driving
once I see it, up the dirt road to the left.
Then right, back into the perfect hills,
back where I've never been.
                 At the gentle curve
up through pasture, there's where the music camp.
The screened porch surrounding the concerts,
the evening surrounding the porch,
the girl with the cello.
                 The car keeps on,
higher, steep right: there's the clear gash
of the ski-jump landing, its natural in-run
a thin cut back into pine.
                 I'm turned around now,
going back down, only my own tracks showing
in the lightest possible snow. It began
when I didn't know, it keeps falling and
falling, as new as if it were April sunlight,
not August,
                 where I slow behind the old theatre,
the white village inn, the deskclerk still a schoolboy,
me wondering if he's held my reservation,
if there's still room for the rest I want,
at least for the rest of this night.

From *Dreams Are Wiser Than Men,* edited by Richard A. Russo (Berkeley, Calif., North Atlantic Books, 1987), 79–85.

Poems after Dreams

It's morning now, coming toward eight on a gray Maine day. I've stoked the woodfire, written in my Dreamlog, walked to the store for the paper, read it, and finished breakfast. I'm up in my second-floor study, about to get down to writing. I begin by looking up old poems of mine which acknowledge dreams as their source. "Night Notes on an Old Dream" (*Paris Review*, 1961), "Fairy Tale" (*Kenyon*, 1963), which reminds me about "Polaris" (*Partisan*, 1957); "Night Figure" (*Shenandoah*, 1965), "A Dream of Russia" (*Poetry Northwest*, 1971), "Dreamscape" (*New Republic*, 1973), and "This Dream" (*Kayak*, 1975). Looking these up I'm simply running my eye down a list, and I see still more poems which remind me how dreams catalyzed their making.

Asked from California yesterday about reprinting "Dreamscape," and if I had any new poems based on dreams, I found myself saying yes to everything. I would even write something about all this, because just this past week I've been working on a new poem called "States" which, like "Dreamscape" much earlier, derives from a specific dream and an actual landscape. Many of my poems are rooted in a specific landscape, and my dreams invariably are, though the dreamscape (however repetitively it appears in various dreams) is usually a lucid distortion of the literal landscape from which it arrives. A friend who'd crossed Russia on the Trans-Siberian Railway in 1940 gave me part of what became the narrative of "A Dream of Russia," for instance, but I later dreamt the landscape as such, and only then began to make it the ground of my poem. "States" geographically presents itself as deriving from the tightly contiguous states of New Hampshire and Vermont, in the first of which I was born and went to college, in the second of which we briefly lived when my wife bore our first two children.

But all of this, so far, is superficial information, exposition which from outside the poem more or less establishes my relationship to the territory of the poem. More or less. I find I haven't said that I was fishing the White River a lot while my wife was bearing, and caring for, brand new daughters. What this may have to do with the poem I can only guess. "States" is in fact too new for me to know how good a poem it may (or *may not*) be; I only know that I liked the process of writing it (though what's here is only its seventh, but probably close to final, draft), and that—asked about "Dreamscape" and other such poems—I'm newly interested in how looking back through a Dreamlog started me writing "States."

One more surface fact: behind me, on a high shelf, are some twelve or fifteen Dreamlogs, spiral notebooks of more or less daily transcriptions of the previous night's dreams. These are altogether separate from my commonplace books, *Fragments,* that I write in with further writing in mind. I've kept notebooks of *Fragments* for at least thirty-five years; I started keeping a Dreamlog some eight or ten years ago, wanting to be more in touch with my inner life, knowing from three-plus years of psychoanalysis in the late 1950s that "wanting to be in touch with my inner life" could be, at times, not only a want but a need. Poems, too, are a need for me, they are one of the necessities of my life.

Writing a poem is for me an act of using language to discover, or at least explore, what I can know about what I feel. And just as I keep a Dreamlog, just as I write my night's dreams down in morning light to illuminate some aspect of my inner life, so am I writing now to find out what I say. Which is to say to find out what I think, what I think about how I feel. In this case about how dreams and poems may relate. That's what I'm trying to write my way down into, down from the surfaces I began on.

I believe, without choice in the matter, in my dreams. I believe my dreams give me some interesting, sometimes even useful, information, differently formed from, but relative to, how poems may inform themselves in the process of being written. Poems and dreams often seem to me to come from the same sea, but on different wavelengths. Very few of my poems depend directly on my dreams, or my experience in interpreting them. I *can* interpret them, but unless one part of my psyche demands to know what some other part is about, I mostly do not interpret them. Analysis taught me (in classically nondirective ways) a lot about interpreting dreams, and a great good lot about not censoring myself; I began to learn, too, at what remove from the dream the report of the dream always is. When I log my dreams now (from whatever scraps of night notes I managed to wake up enough to scrawl), I know that I'm already informing (though not necessarily "censoring") the dream in ways that are definitively different from how it structured itself as I slept. I've read very little psychoanalytic theory, and am not inclined to: I don't want to be burdened by theory as I wake to report to myself as much as I can of the dream I slept my way into. What I report the dream was *is* what the dream was: it has no other being for me at the moment in which I write.

The problem with logging dreams is to avoid formal interpretation as such, and to write them as soon after dreaming (and as quickly) as possible, in whatever sequence their parts arrive at one's pen. But the primary problem precedes even that: to remember one's dreams at all. As Jerome Bruner says somewhere in *On Knowing,* the problem of information is "not storage but retrieval." Precisely. And here the relation between logging dreams and writing poems is acutely apparent. All of us know how often we dream what we don't wake up to remember; any of us who are poets know the more painfully how many poems we begin in the dark never get to a daylit page. The crucial time, whether in darkness or partial or full light, is the time when one's conscious self starts to wake. In the demimonde of waking resides, I suspect, the source of my own best poems, whether or not they immediately derive from dreams. Roethke's great line, "I wake to sleep and take my waking slow," speaks marvellously for a lifetime; whether it should be taken as a prescription for retrieving one's dreams or mid-night poems probably depends on one's metabolism. How one recovers dreams, or recovers from them, or retrieves poems, historically has much to do with one's so-called mental health; it has no less to do with the vital nature of one's work. Nobody ever said it better than William Empson:

> From partial fires
> The waste remains, the waste remains and kills.
> It is the poems you have lost, the ills

From missing dates, at which the heart expires.
Slowly the poison the whole blood stream fills.
The waste remains, the waste remains and kills.

With luck, I can, on some mornings, recall parts (I'd like to think wholes) of seven or eight dreams. The Dreamlog entry that catalyzed "States" is more lucid than most, one of two entries for the night in question. I found it months later when I was, literally, re-searching my Dreamlog for information that has nothing to do with the entry or with poems. Here's the log of that dream, verbatim:

> *In little village (like above Royalton on E branch of W. River) there's what used to be the famous little town theatre. I drive by that, think of buying it; then drive behind and up left, turning right into the hills (like* back *of Moose Mtn related to some Northern NH DS but new) where I've never been. Bleak, beautiful (like behind Velvet Rocks but more so); I go on by another former music house and sort of long chalet/barracks for the music camp; and up behind, to the steep right, there's then a clear cut gash for the not so little ski-jump w. natural in-run. Lovely, the snow barely limning the hard ground, and then I drive slightly down to the left, and up a valley where only the* light *new (now falling) snow shows the two tracks. But the road begins to fade out, track runs out, and I see that it is, surprisingly, six-o-clock (pm), so I turn around and drive back past the little buildings, remote and empty in the lovely village square.*

The dream was more joyful for me than the log shows. The dream is clear on its own terms. My logging it obviously involved my interest in how the dreamscape reflected literal places (a Vermont town, then two very small New Hampshire mountains, the first of which reminded me of some distantly related dreamscape); I wrote a single sentence of interpretation after I'd recorded the dream, and I starred in the margin the phrase "where I've never been," the part about the ski-jump, and the part about the two tracks. The idea of my wanting to buy a theatre astounds me; on any daylight list of mine, that possibility would be close to the bottom of the page, perhaps just above moving to Outer Mongolia. I cannot pretend to interpret every element of the dream now, nor could I then; in the context of the particular morning I wrote it down I would (and did, briefly) interpret it differently from how I now might. I am not going to interpret it now. You who read this may interpret it as you please. But without context the dream is marvellously abstract. Whatever you may bring to it will be more important to you than to me, even as my knowledge of its context, and—say—my experience as a ski-jumper some thirty and forty years ago is important to how I read the dream. If you knew that I'd talked just the night before this dream to a man just back from Murmansk (the man, coincidentally, who long ago told me about riding the Trans-Siberian Railway), you might be foolishly inclined to relate my poem "A Dream of Russia" to this particular poem. But you still would not know what that old jumper said to me one March morning thirty years ago on the out-run of a small Vermont jump. And I, who am clearly baiting the large possibility of irrelevant interpretation, am not now going to leap to that tangential information. You may have noticed, as I just now did, that my negative sense of "moving to Outer Mongolia" apparently foreshadowed my friend's returning from Murmansk, and my returning to his experience on the Trans-Siberian Railway; those associations, however apparently casual, seem to me to be valid. But consider how differently one might interpret my dream if one knew that I long ago gashed my leg in a bad fall on a ski-jump, and that only a week before this dream I had spent the night in an emergency room as the result of a car accident that fractured my leg. No, neither accident is true. So neither signifies, not even now, not in interpreting the dream.

Nor does either red-herring signify in reading the poem I've called "States," a poem into which I've built some clearly limiting contexts. I'm inventing this bad bait about injury only in the context of writing down my suspicions of interpretive theory. My primary concern, here, is not interpretation or theory, but what may be for a poet the practical relation between two aspects of imagination. The dream and the poem came out of the same sea, yes; but the dream is still free-floating in primordial ways, and the poem, no less instinctually, seems to want to establish its own territory on the littoral.

Dream and poem (this dream, this poem) are relative in that both are imaginative events. And insofar as the poem in this case contains, like human blood, about the same salinity as the sea even though it is less fluid than the dream, it's maybe worth recalling that the chief proverb of Biology I, "Ontogeny recapitulates phylogeny," applies also to poetics. The clearest distinction between dream and poem is, for me, the ways in which they are structured, which is to say *how* each one is informed. The poem is to the Dreamlog report as the Dreamlog report is to the dream. Event by event, each has fallen into consciousness. Or, perhaps, climbed into consciousness. Either way, Heraclitus is still right about "The way up and the way down. . . . " Yet I'm clear in my mind that the structuring of a poem is more rather than less conscious: the poet-as-structurer is, obviously, more constructive than the poet-as-dreamer. However constructive therapeutically a dream may be in providing material for analysis, or simply in having been dreamt, the dream-in-itself may be what, in a "picture of Picasso's," Stevens understood as "this 'hoard / Of destructions,' a picture of ourselves . . . "

A dream, arriving in sleep apparently ex nihilo, can make present the *something* from which, out of which, a poem can be made. The dream's latent energies can make possible the manifest poem. The poet cannot choose to dream or not dream. The poet cannot choose the nature of the dream, which, before all, is dreamt *by* the poet-as-dreamer not *for* the poet-as-poet. The poem the poet writes is for reading and hearing, it opens itself to making manifest what's latent, explicit what's implicit, to the degree the poet wishes or can emotionally and tactically realize. The dream, as such, is selfish; the poem, as such, is an act of sharing. To what extent a poem need make its meaning explicit, and how it may make its emotions felt, are strategic and tactical problems with which any poet's work must constantly concern itself. Witness Stevens, seventeen sections beyond his mention of Picasso in " . . . The Blue Guitar": "Throw away the lights, the definitions, / And say of what you see in the dark // That it is this or that it is that, / But do not use the rotted names." For my own part, not wanting to use names long since rotted or names newly rotten, I can only say that unless a poem keeps emotional contact with its latent content (whether the energies of that content present themselves in sleep or wakefulness), no amount of manifest content can bring, or keep, the poem alive. It will lack, as a poem, the rhythms, the syntactical tensions, and a verbal contact with the unsayable, that are its vital signs.

I discover, surfacing again, that writing this assay has temporarily displaced the poem that catalyzed it. Perhaps the poem is less vital than I hoped it was before I started writing around and about it. Or perhaps I've self-deflected the poem by being consciously self-conscious about the process of moving to poem from dream. Yeats offers large-scale examples of such imaginative movement, mine is simply one example among many others. But I dislike finding in this prose a degree of self-consciousness that distantly echoes a greater self-consciousness, even a pretentiousness, that I much dislike in Yeats' theorizing about his own sources. At least in prose. When he's less abstract about those sources, as he is in "The Circus Animals' Desertion" when he talks about Cuchulain & Co., I'm the more happily convinced:

> . . . yet when all is said
> It was the dream itself enchanted me:
> Character isolated by a deed
> To engross the present and dominate memory.

After all, it's the poem that matters. After all. In my own present experience the dream is long gone, the logged dream is inconsequentially private; the poem is (or will be) finally itself, an individual act that may prove to be an imaginative event, a poem that may validate, and deepen, a reader's sense of such human experience as we inevitably share. Not this poem "States," perhaps, but perhaps some further poem which owes to something I came to feel or realize in writing "States." The states of dream and poem are contiguous, as tightly joined and separated as New Hampshire and Vermont are by the complex windings of the Connecticut River.

What I have written here is an assay of the relation between a poem and *one* of its possible sources. A dream which simply "came to me" catalyzed a poem which, by active and conscious choice on my part, assimilated into its being some of the dream. The dream gave me access to feelings I didn't remember I'd felt, to images I didn't know I'd known. The problem of writing poems invariably involves such access, whether or not such access involves a dream. The problem of writing a poem, a truly original poem, not just a mass-produced look-alike, involves being open to the demand(s) of "the voice . . . within us," the voice that bespeaks the presence of poetry in the dailiness of our lives. The voice that ("great" or not) is as surely a given as any night's dream. The problem of writing poems is not time or (up to a point) energy; the constant problem is to remain open to the possibility of poems. And after that to sustain the imaginative energy which catalyzed the poem. Whatever catalyzed the poem, dream or no, remains (by definition) unchanged; but the poem can change if it is written in ways that give it a chance to grow. A dream is never conclusive, yet ends; a poem is conclusive only temporarily, perhaps over and over. Perhaps, vitally, Frost's "momentary stay against confusion."

Momentary as the stay may be, we need it as poets, we need as poets to share it with readers. Not to explain, as John Peale Bishop explained, but to illuminate. To cast light, even on the dark of our dreams or on a light snowfall in August Vermont. And what may such examples show? I think of Delmore Schwartz's first great title, *In Dreams Begin Responsibilities,* and I steal from the penultimate question of his "For the One Who Would Take Man's Life in His Hands," to let him ask that question and—for many of us, asleep or awake—answer it:

> —What do all examples show?
> What can any actor know?
> The contradiction in every act,
> The infinite task of the human heart.

Selected "Fragments," 1961

From the four-hundred-some entries I wrote between June 1960 and November 1965 in the spiral notebook that is a thin Volume IV in the series of such notebooks I began in 1950 as Fragments, *the following twenty-five entries come from a five-month period exactly thirty years ago.*

These entries begin with part of a July-end letter I wrote to an oldest friend the day after I "interrupted" the three-and-a-half years of psychoanalysis which coincided with my final seven semesters of teaching at Wellesley. During July I had taught with John Holmes in his Tufts Poetry Workshop. I went home to Maine for three weeks before moving in September to begin teaching at Syracuse in what would become the Writing Program I was hired to help get started.

That this series of entries untypically includes parts of five letters is, I now think, only one measure of how I was trying to reassure myself, and to write my way out *of what, for me, was a miserable transition inland. I was, during the summer and fall of 1961, a man hired as a poet who had no poems in him. I had yet to commute back to Boston for intermittent therapy; I had yet to learn from living Upstate the glory of "upland light / fallen through miles of trees."*

❧

To D[avid] B[radley], July 29: Such partings are, I suspect, known only to old lovers; it's both like a funeral and being reborn. The wound that woman-surgeon helped me open saved me from something very much like death; I hate her guts for hurting me so, and love her for the healing she has started in my own. Nobody who has not been through it can

---

From *Seneca Review* 21, no. 2 (Spring 1992).

know, I truly think. . . . One grows up, maybe, on just such Guadalcanals, and forever knows that no civilian words can get the battle said, or tell what happened when the tracers arc'd in close. One is not cured or much changed, only re-inforced where it counts most by having submitted to the battle itself, and having survived. No medals, no merit badges, no report cards, no engraved graduation certificate. But I suddenly, this first day when the guns are strangely quiet, am like Kilroy: somewhere back in the jungle there is a tree ini-tialled by my knife. I was there. I hope like Christ never to have to return. But I was there; and having been, and come through, gives me, at the very least, more than a fighting chance at not having to go back.

🐾

THE COLD COAST

a book of the year's round as
the year turns (with *people*) in Castine.

🐾

August: Phil Perkins [Castine's unofficial historian] says that Holman Day was "the poet laureate of Maine, writing about those 'degenerates' in a little town up around Hebron."

🐾

August 23: 7 beers, 1 whiskey, 3 gin and tonics, one glass of wine and 1 brandy.

🐾

Cal [Lowell], of a breakfast with Jerry [Bruner] and Blanche [Marshall], says that I've "made it" with *The Islanders*. He says that it's "rooted in real earth," that "there's all sorts of solid ver-sification," and that I've staked out Castine as my own (in oppo-sition to the sort of *use* I made of Maine stuff in *Letter* . . .). The endings, he says, "are different from how I write; they have a kind of dying fall except in poems like 'Propeller.' " He liked the first and last poems ("the right one to end with") especially, also the other "right" ones like "The Owl" and "Propeller" and—surprisingly—"The Anchor." Least of all: "Painter" and "The Round"; but admiration of variousness of prosody, "the WmCWms short-line ones (like 'The Tower') and the long-line ones like 'Jake's Wharf'—one of your best." The tone was what he appeared to like best, "the somewhat hortatory—not exactly this, but this"—flatness and flexibility.

&

September: Syracuse-Fayetteville [311 Salt Springs Road]: I'm homesick already and, looking back through these fragments to find old things, it strikes me that the repetitive notes for still unwritten pieces are useful only if to be written *away from* into fictions of which these fragments only define a tone.

&

Thrumcap

&

Pip, Ahab's, as Olson rightly sees him: a poem in his own right.

&

THE TOYS, as in July '55, and the impossibility of freeing the frozen wheel. Black tractor, blue wrecker, green bus: the castiron halves pinned. The woodshed attic.

&

Not being able to see the North Star.

&

[Dream]: The big attack on the Castine house. Images of camp (John Moir), V[ermont] A[cademy] ("Tex"), and the fear of losing skis and lack of police protection. The local teddyboys, E[xxxx] C[xxxxx] *et al*, take room after room.

&

How ironies compound.

&

Consider: how many poems *La Dolce Vita* makes it unnecessary to write, Fellini's camera having already done that work; yet how many more poems, against the chaos of this very life, the movie demands.

ॐ

Quoted in a letter from J[ohn] H[olmes]: "A writer is a man alone in a room with the English language."

ॐ

Names of Islands:	*Ledges:*
Pond	The Brown Cow
Hog	Ship and Barges
Butter	Otter Rock
Sprucehead	Stone Horse
Horsehead	
Colthead	
Thrumcap	
Ram	
Sheep	
The Virgin's Breasts	
Pumpkin	
Two Bush	
Birch	

ॐ

October: Am I not in too close touch to a lesser reality?

ॐ

In answer to Charles Olson, October 14: My purpose, as best I know to say it, is only to use right words to define the perhaps meaning of a world I want to love, and to establish some structure of language which—as accurately as possible—reflects my sense of the relationships implicit in that world's superficial disorder. I have to revise even here: I'm trying to talk about poetry as re-seeing, about re-seeing as a way of sensing the world's poetry.

A different language makes, *by definition,* a different kind of statement. Compare the language of Wilbur's "Mind," say, with the language of Denise Levertov's "Matins."

But the language depends, primarily and irrevocably, on the sense of *time* that underlies and is our major sense of relationship.

I wanted oceans where I lived, a coast to look out somewhere from. Homing here, I came home lost—the Milky Way its own sea and all that, but there are no passages offshore *on my own plane.* That's what haunts me about the Bay: my knowledge there is of headlands, islands, ledges, which are landmarks for how one tacks through them. *Permit Me Voyage* was one great title!

To be well is unlikely; to live well is impossible. To feel well is an absurd possibility, but to think well one can learn.

Today's only the 24th, and I already disagree with part of what I wrote Olson a week ago.

From a letter to Signe Clutz [Wellesley '62]: Don't worry about diving in. Most poetry gets written underwater anyway, at about that level where what's light above filters down into the dark below.

To Ben[son] Snyder [M.D.], December 18: It seems to me that Freud (and all his followers and non-followers) learned deeply from what poets (in the general sense of the word) have written as tragedies: *Oedipus, Hamlet, Lear,* and so on. And that, as all analysts—from Freud's concern with Irma's Injection to The Botanical Monograph, etc.—have been terrifyingly involved in potential tragedy, they tend to write about analysis with a necessarily defensive dispassion which Sophocles or Shakespeare neither needed nor wanted. Tragedy deals dramatically in fatal *acts*. But analysis, a drama without action, is a *comedy*. Did I not weep, hate, love, get gut-struck, and shake until I was cold? I did. Did I not imagine that I had caused my mother's death by violating a prime taboo, and that I could or would kill my father to earn my way free of such violation? I did. But somehow, in retrospect, it seems to me that I continually could see myself *pretending* to those acts of tragic consequence. As Dr. F. continually reinforced what I suppose was my ego, she kept such sight in my mind. But was it not fundamentally *comic* that I imagined that I was *unique* in imagining such tragic possibilities? The tragic hero, *acting* on his sense of uniqueness, *acts* to create tragedy (tragedy because he has partial self-knowledge). But to realize that one is not unique (in wanting, masochistically, as a martyr, to act on such impulse) is to see one's self as fool protagonist in a comedy of errors. Analysis, in truth, is the world's greatest and most lonely comedy; analysts (and ex-analysands who, still identifying, wish they were analysts) will write well about analysis only when they learn to laugh with (not at) themselves and their patients. What madness (literally) it is to believe that one is *uniquely* committed to murder and incest. But what a saving grace it is, in whatever painful comedy, to realize that so to feel capable of acting (without *having* to act) is to join the human race. Do we lose our unique individuality in so admitting we are human? Hardly. We begin, I begin to find, to give up wasting *this* sense of uniqueness in order to be unique in the meaningfully mature ways of which we are humanly capable.

&

From a letter to J[ames] W[right], December 27 [which refers to "First Draft," a poem in *The Islanders*]: If a few of us don't survive, none of us will. We are bound, in spite of the fools we are, by the words we risk being true to. "The late fog, lifting" is a sentence, and it sentences us to be true to the pure fact we can learn to act on. Myths, as they were true for the one man who wrote them, become the factual basis of how we learn to live. Fiction they may be, but they state a truth truer than so-called non-fiction will ever know. The world is a poem, as my poem to you tried to get said, and we can only write it by cutting away the prose as a sculptor chips at stone to discover the figure the grain of the stone contains. I think we marry that figure, and I think, if we will, we write ourselves into the truth we've pared away falsehood to find.

Selected "Fragments," 1987

These notebook entries come from my most recent volume of Fragments, *a series of spiral-bound commonplace books I've been keeping for (and to) myself since 1950. These twenty-eight entries (of the three-hundred-some written in 1987) come from typically various sectors of my interests at the time. I selected these present entries in the sequence they appear, unedited; it seemed to me that they come to some temporary conclusion with the first draft of what became a poem called "Calling."*

Though "Calling" involves many of the realms these entries, in retrospect, search their way into, I've never thought of such entries as "work-in-progress"; I continue to think of them only as disparate (and all but aleatory) measures of a lifetime given to writing-as-process. I'm in no way an "experimental writer" if, as I think, experiments are devised to prove a preconception. These fragments are nothing if not pragmatic. They were written at odd times, mostly quickly, in my need to shape experience, to give experience language, to find ways of giving language some life of its own. Uneven as they are, they have been for me, for years, a way of serving my apprenticeship to myself.

from Fragments

Do, don't own.
Live with, not for.
Love to give;
give to, not for.
Give to love.
Love, don't own.

🍃

1

From *Ploughshares* 17, no. 1 (May 1991).

Make *music,* however minor the key, however subtle the chord.   9

&.

    Not to be Jesus the infant; not of course Christ;
    but Christopher, old Christopher, lugging the child
    across, his sink-stick cracked, yet useful for
                    feeling the way.   23

&.

      Reading Santayana at 3 A.M.,
      storm rain come suddenly on the dormer,
      its music as vital as Bach, I think
      I feel for the moment as peaceful as
      Plato must have felt once.   25

&.

    A man named Mann came to the door
    of the world, and opened himself to entering.   27

&.

      The iron smell of snow going to come. West
      of here now, but out there, already falling.   35

&.

Muse, museum, music I guessed I knew, but *mosaic* surprised me.   43

&.

The last sentence of Cees' new book, "I sat there happily ever after," would be greatly more interesting were it "I sat there. Happily. Ever after."   54

&.

Washington dead, Boston dying; much of the country ill; this state being violated, this village being taken over by people vainly insecure, ignorant by choice, greedy beyond belief. 83

&.

To think of what she carried, *how,* her belly swelled until her navel popped inside out, as if it might remind her of the

mother she was attached to, and *her* mother . . . mothers all,
all mothers, down through generations.   *98*

જ

Poetry is important enough to die for; more important, to live
for. And, like music, with.   *116*

જ

> What if. When if.
> If I die they
> will be gone to
>
> me. Forever.
> Best not soon.   *135*

જ

> I want to warm you,
> you told me. I want
> you to. Why don't you
> then you said, *you,*
> hold me. Enfold me.   *137*

જ

> The glory of the world, the physics
> of the world within my eye,
> the wonder of the mind it patterns.   *143*

જ

> Winters aren't bad, it's the men get harsh.
> Hard boys at fifteen, quick fathers
> at twenty, their faces begin to freeze before
> they melt with liquor.   *151*

જ

Being a poet is not a career, it's a life. Writing poems is not a
career but a lifetime of looking into, and listening to, how
words see.

    Except as a kind of apprenticeship, poetry is not what one
tries to write; one has, being moved by it, to try to write the
world, and so move it.

You must let the poem speak to you; you must let the poem
tell you how it wants to be. Your being is already part of what
the poem is coming to be; its being is continually part of who
you are as you open yourself to write.   *152*

ẽæ

All writing is a closing off and an opening; even within a
poem these pressures and relaxations show themselves in how
the poem moves, how it paces itself.   *153*

ẽæ

Dost think, because thou art withering,
that none of the rest of us are growing old.   *163*

ẽæ

Time out of mind. Mind out of time.
Mind out of synch with *what,* if not time.
I am timesick when I worry about hurrying,
    about the calendar on the wall, or I
    am timesick when I am worried that I
    am ill, or am going to be ill,
    perhaps terminally. In which case time
    will go on without me. Is time always
    without me, when I feel it internally?
All is not well with a mind that is sick of time.
Time is the/a (?) sequence of cosmic events
    through which we live daily lives looking
    at the hour and minute hands of our watches.
    Or the second hand, if we count our pulse
    as beating too fast.
We perceive time at different rates, life by
    life, person by person, day by day—which
    is itself a temporal measure even as it
    is a temporal metaphor. Of survival, not least.
I cannot believe I am so many years old, that
    I have lived so long a time.
Not a day passes but I wonder about how much
    time I have.   *164*

ẽæ

A bay of islands rimmed by mountains.   *166*

☙

A single great mare's tail, a mile wide over me, spiraled one
and a half times back beyond the Camden Hills to a whole
horizon bright with fair-weather cumulus.   *168*

☙

~~the faintest wind~~
~~the slightest wind~~
the lightest wind   *169*

☙

This side of flight, what densities
they inhabit: mergansers, diving, plovers
dipping their beaks to the tide edge.   *170*

☙

At his father's interment wind washed away what he'd tried to
get said.   *188*

☙

And in Mongolia the days without a tree, the weeks, the bright-
ness of the wind across the plain, the miles of light in which a
rabbit rises, magnified. And, shot, regresses and regresses
when you ride to pick him up. And trees, *the* tree, seems small
for half a day then looms like two small yaks.   *189*

☙

The lines apparently open, but more actually hermetic, as
they hold the syntax closed to all who cannot open themselves
to reading—as it happens—both ways at once.   *194*

☙

The nature of Dorset carving, according to Canadian art
critic George Swinton, "exudes intensity and power . . . de-
spite its subtlety and delicacy." Their form "emphasizes con-
tent, vigour, and involvement (as opposed to style, elegance,
and detachment)."
          —after Barry Lopez, *Arctic Dreams*, p. 182   *208*

&

Under the heavy Northwest sky,
a single strip of deep light, leaving
the day to early dark. ✝A man looks
at his watch: 4:33. In another
twenty-~~seven~~ some minutes, he thinks,
the rates will be cheap. And for
the first time in fourteen years
since he died, he thinks
~~I mean~~ *I'm going to phone father.*

—13 XI 87   *255*

101

Lives We Keep Wanting to Know

Interview by Richard Jackson, 1978

Cézanne once remarked that his aim was to retrieve objects from behind the atmosphere impressionists drew over them. To do so, he said, he had to become part of the landscape: "The landscape thinks itself in me and I am its consciousness." One could begin to discuss your work by talking about its descriptive quality, that is, the nature of perception for you, the relation between the literal and the figural, the concrete object and the (subjective) image of the object. For example, in "How to See Deer," you seem on one level to prescribe a literal "See / What you see," and you take a similar stance in "Adding It Up." But the poems are obviously more than literal descriptions—as a poem like "Stove," where a whole narrative background is revealed as part of the meaning of the image of the stove. In all your poems, there is a way in which the world enters you as you enter it—perspectives blend. In "Let the Trees," you say, "let your two eyes / fill them, even as then / your own two eyes may / be filled," playing on the poem on "eye" and "I."

In terms of the action of the poem, perception is very often visual. And also very often narrative in the sense that the "I" of the poem sees things in a certain sequence which then comes to some consequence—what the poem is about. I suppose I think with Stevens that description is revelation, but that the revelation from my point of view is the result of relationships, whether those relationships are as simple as between cataloged names or as complex as the ambivalence of

From *The Poetry Miscellany* no. 8 (1978): 21–26.

objects and subjects as one perceives them. I think of myself basically as a namer; I continue to think of Adam as the first poet. I want to pare away excess detail toward a kind of essential specificity which may in itself, as the objects and subjects interrelate, come to a kind of revelation.

One way I might answer your question is to say that the poet doesn't choose his subjects or forms, that they, in effect, choose him. I think of myself as a participating observer; I don't think of the poem as a story coldly told, but I probably have a built-in New England reticence that I come by honestly. I like and admire Maine talk in its most laconic aspects. There's a great deal of selection that goes on when I write because I revise a lot. But I'm always after an illusion of spontaneity no matter how tight-lipped the poem may be.

Could you expand on your sense of the "narrative" element you have alluded to here? It seems refreshingly broad.

Narrative depends on the sequence in which things are described—be they events, or images of objects, or states of being. I don't think of description for its own sake as being fundamental. I want to pare away anything that is merely ornamental—to get at an essence. That starkness is for me a way to let objects or emotions illuminate themselves. It is in the relationship between them that the event of the poem or the event of the metaphor occurs. They operate in time. I prefer a definition of narrative that includes Frost's "Neither Out Far Nor in Deep" as well as "Home Burial." Obviously, I do not write many straight narratives; probably "A Dream of Russia" is as straight a narrative as I have. But almost every poem implies a narrative to me in some way.

And in that poem, "A Dream of Russia," the plot unfolds in a "tight-lipped" manner, and it comes to a reticent close.

I like the kind of stories I hear almost every day on the wharf here. They are almost always circular or egg-shaped, and they often come out to one word. Here is an almost literal transcription of what I heard last July fifth. A young fisher-man and an older fisherman are talking on the wharf after the weekend of the Fourth. The younger worker says: "What d'ya do over the Fourth—go out an' get drunk?" The older one takes a long time to answer, then he says, "Nope." An-other long pause. The younger one says, "Didn't go out an' get drunk?" Another pause—"Nope." Then the younger one says, "Well, what didya do?" Another pause—"Stayed home." Then, after a while, "Suppose ya got drunk there." Then, finally, "Yup." And that's the whole story. I like its pace, its understatement.

The shortness, the tightness of your lines provides you with the basic technique to achieve this pace.

I have sometimes wanted to write longer lined poems, but they generally come out in meters that don't interest me any-more. Merleau-Ponty has an essay on the gestalt of film, the rate it reveals itself, which agrees with my concern with pace. The poem can't get started for me unless I feel it in motion. I think a poem begins with an image—I work from the simple image or the juxtaposed image—but unless I can get that moving, unless I can get some motion to it, it falters. For me, it's a matter of the rhythm of the phrase, the syncopation against that of how the line-end works, and finally the pace of the whole poem.

Do you sense the rhythm before you begin?

No, I don't hear it in the abstract, but unless I hear the rhythm in the words the poem is bound to go wrong. I remember when I first began to write I was subverted for months by the first line of Richard Wilbur's poem "He Was," which uses the title to enter the text: "a brown old man with a green thumb." I feel very strongly that in the kinds of poems I write the line defines a great deal of what the rhythm comes to. I hear the caesura that comes with the break, the slash that's given when you quote, the hold you get in the double sense of both "wait" and "weight."

When you get going does the rhythm tend to steer the poem?

No, I don't think it does, though I don't want the poem to lose that original impulse. When I say impulse I'm getting back to the possibility of a pulse, some undercurrent, some underbeat. But I want the poem to be able to shift gears rhythmically as, say, Charles Ives can change his measure in the process of a piece. I don't mean just a slowing down, but changing the time in which the poem operates. The poem is written in time to see what the poem outside time comes to.

This notion of catching, or to use your word from earlier, receiving the rhythm and then changing it, or receiving an image that then is juxtaposed to others rhythmically, perhaps altering its context, could be related to what we were saying earlier about perception—the relation of the perceiver to his world.

Absolutely, and I think that as a poet you are necessarily changing the world. I think that we all want to modify our world so that we are not merely photographing it. The title *Available Light* plays on that possibility of photographic reproduction, which nevertheless involves selection, depth of focus, depth of field. I think that Auden is wrong; poetry *does* make something happen. It makes the world more habitable. To make the world more habitable you build constructs in it, from it. The world is the more revealed, to go back to our original word, from the relationships that enter into the construct. So I do think of the poet as a maker as well as a namer. For me, the making function is superior to the naming function, not morally, but in the level of construction that's going on. Unless a poem does move, unless it has that motion we were talking about, it is not going to move the reader. I want the poem to move the reader off the page, not so much to extend the reader's perceptions as to "subtlize" them, as Melville says. One of the things I like about Maine speech, Maine laconics, is that you have to, living on the edge of things, between land and sea, treat things for what they are and sense the ambivalence in them without trying to build a program around it.

I wonder to what extent you think of the metaphoric "impulse" of poetry as essentially ambivalent. Metaphor involves a crossing over or transformation of the two juxtaposed terms, as you've described. It occurs as a blending in a more direct to extreme way in a poem like "The Owl," where you do exchange consciousness with the bird—and can thus proclaim at the end, "I begin to see," referring to sight in its various senses. In personal terms, any such exchange of consciousness is very difficult, if not impossible, as in "Lives," where one is always searching for "lives / we keep wanting to know." The aim seems to be to see things two ways at once.

I think that the end of "Lives" that you quote comes very close to the ambivalence I'm looking for, a kind of perfectly balanced ambivalence. I don't want to say equipoise because that seems too static, but equal in tension. For instance, I understand those last lines to say both "lives we keep wanting to know us, in the sense of our situation," and "lives we keep wanting to know as we reach out to touch them." I want the space on the page, I want the line-breaks, to invite the reader in that direction, to slow the reader down to that kind of ambivalence. A newer poem, which talks about people asleep in a village, ends, "people I cannot help love." Of course I mean it in the sense of the cliché, but also in the sense that I am helpless to help them love. Both these cases are fair instances of the kinds of ambivalence that I want the poems to make clear. We come back to "made" in the sense that the poem has to be "made" to make that happen. So one way to answer your question is to say that though I'm interested in the metaphoric in all its senses, probably my poems have become less metaphorical in the sense of conventional metaphor. I don't particularly aim for this, but I'm tired of, for instance, the kind of metaphor that is so programmatic and which is such a burden to the so-called deep image poets; I'm tired of what passes for surrealism and is so formulaic for the third and fourth generation "surrealist." My rule of thumb is "Honor thy subject in whatever complexity of perception is necessary." If I can make that perception clearly simple or simply clear so that both terms show equally, I'm happy, for it reflects my sense of the doubleness of vision we have. Always it's one thing in terms of another. If there is to be any revelation, it has to come from the relationship which by definition posits a doubleness.

Of course, you are distinguished from the "surrealists" by your overt consciousness and control, the distance your "I" often achieves from a scene. Still, more of your poems in Available Light *are dream poems than in any previous book. Keeping in mind this doubleness, this controlled ambivalence you've been describing, could you talk about the role of the unconscious and the irrational in poetry? What, for example, makes a detail relevant? Freud describes the way the primary process is a wandering of meaning onto what might have been irrelevant details. Can there be an open-ended play between objects as determiners of meaning and objects as part of the world, between our inner drives to make something of the world and the world in which we find ourselves? The irrelevant detail takes on some meaning, for Freud, just by its context; could you see the poem as marking an emergence of form against the closure of the structure?*

This is exactly what happens in psychoanalysis; if the analysand can't free himself, if he has so much control he cannot let his Id go, not much is going to happen from the process. It seems to me that the wandering of meanings that goes on in psychoanalysis is something discernibly different from stream of consciousness. When you begin to deal with a single dream which may in itself undergo all sorts of condensation in the Freudian sense, but also may undergo editorializing, cutting in the sense of writing—when the dream undergoes these processes, it is because the writer has more of an inkling of how the latent content shows through the manifest content. I've kept some dream logs myself in difficult times, and I've found that only by waking myself up at night could I get the dream down; and then, only by getting down to the dream again in the morning could I begin to see the latent meanings coming through the manifest content. I think this process vastly extended happens in the poem. The poet is more in control because he is consciously revising; and that also means to envision the original vision. He isn't censoring the dream in the classic sense.

I used to be inclined to do what one of my students, Larry Levis, calls "tuck the poem under at the end." I'm now inclined to leave it more open-ended, more ambivalent. The horizon or edge or margin seems more terrifying now, but more wonderful. The margins themselves seem narrower, but within that narrowness I want to be able to look both ways, up and down, in and out.

Are there points in the process at which you say about an image or even a line, "I don't know why that's there but I know it should be there"?

Sure, and a great deal of revision in the process of making the poem is for me to discover what those potential meanings are and to help the poem as a whole move toward some resolution of them. I don't mean a forcing of them to come to some consequence, but seeing in a sequence if they do come to some consequence. I don't want those phrases or code words to show finally in the poem, as such, but to have them integrated into the total meaning of the poem, the total flow of the poem.

Can this be seen as a tension between finished surface and original depth? I think this is playfully explored in "Strata." But take the poem "Photographer," where the poet goes to the depth of things in order to find "Shapes, pulsing" that can be captured. Perhaps the paradigmatic poem, though, is "Heart of Darkness," where the poet aims toward the "elusive" center, and the poem that would at that point "map the bottom" of things as "some sort of base / to start from"— which "might / enlarge our harlequin / mind." The perceived object is often like that—a center, a depth, a starting point from which an area of concerns can be mapped.

It's a question of both where the poem starts from and where it comes to. Marlowe goes into the darkness following Kurtz. There is a part of any poet that takes him down into that part of himself where he would not otherwise go. I think that maybe the center, what you call the center, the depth, is inherently, implicitly what the poem starts from although it doesn't know it yet. Now, I want to go back to what you said about description. I do want an absolute clarity on the surface, and I want that surface of the poem not to mask the depths in any way, but to enable those depths to be revealed at a rate appropriate to the complexity of the seeing, of the looking in, of the looking down. I don't think a poem like "Photographer" satisfies me very much now, whereas "Snapshots from Kentucky" gives itself more opportunities through its screwy syntax and juxtapositions. The photographs in that poem are tied together in an imagined narrative, making a story as if the voice were telling about them as apocalyptic events.

Another way we could talk about this movement, the relation of the center to the unfolding poem, is in terms of time. In "Moment," time is a relentlessly linear progression, and moments must be perceived before they die, the focus being on the "now." And in "Graffito," "Time is nature's way / of preventing / everything / from happening all at once." But in other poems the moment is insufficient. I think the poem you referred to, "Snapshots from Kentucky," plays off what is captured on the photo against the narratives behind it, linking it to others in a very sophisticated manner. And in "Dark," the moment is defined by what is beyond it—"six months from now / to the moment," to be precise.

In "Dark," various images provide for the speaker an access to the future, to the existence of a future, so that the moment in which the poem finds itself becomes part of a continuum which he can project. In "Moment," the process of the poem involves coming to an access of that moment itself. There is a more happy sense of the immediate moment than there is in "Dark," and I think that the distance between them accurately measures the movement of *Available Light.*

The structure of Available Light *is fascinating. At the beginning, a speaker seems encased in literal or metaphoric winter scenes, looking out, and when he sometimes gets out, as in "The Winter of Separation," it is to be brought back in; at the end, the process is reversed, and the couple skating on the ice are looking at the world under the ice as if trying to get in. They are trying to get at a source, but a source that is found at the end of the book. The whole book is structured on these details or ambivalences, as you've called the relation of ins and outs. And it progresses from that enclosed world, to the freer world of the dream poems, to a continually expanding world.*

Would that all readers were as good as you. I don't presume to see all of those movements going on in the book, but I do intuit them to a certain degree. I put the book together in something like that direction. This does not mean that every poem bears on every other one. The epigraph from Karl Jaspers speaks to what the content is in large terms: "Being itself comes out of all origins to meet me. I myself am given to myself . . . . In losing the substance of my self I sense Nothingness. In being given to myself I sense the fullness . . . I can only maintain my integrity, can prepare, and can remember." This is the nature of the margin on which the book operates.

Jaspers talks somewhere about his aim as being a phenomenological description of the fringes of our experienced world. The margin, in terms of the ambivalence you talked about earlier, is a kind of threshold, isn't it?

I think that about amounts to it—a threshold to what, one does not know except to say that it's always a threshold to death. My poems more and more sense life as a contingent process, the contingency enters into the poems not only in poems like "Panic," but also in the sense of the various contingencies we face through our consciousness of the possible ways of dying. There is the deepening watch on one's mortality in the poem called "Watch," and the valuing of that moment in the poem called "Moment," for what it is in its own rather than what it leads to. All these elements are more strong in my work now than they were.

Some of your poems have that sense that Jaspers describes of going beyond the boundary, but not in any transcendental way. In that space beyond is a strange, indescribable existence, not really free, not quite limited. "Voyages" describes it as an imaginative journey. Some of the mystery, and that's the best word I can think of, is brought out in "The Islanders," where there is an island that exists beyond the boat's cruis-

ing "limits" and remains an enigma. More recently, "It Is Being" speaks in more philosophic terms about what it means to be—a going beyond the horizon to this mysterious world.

There's an acceptance of being there, an acceptance of inhabiting that space—without much choice. That is, I suppose that in the process of such poems, the poem comes to discover that there is not much choice, that the movement of the poem is toward this end which is an end yet not a stasis, at least in the poem. I don't think of horizons themselves as limits because they move with us. Jaspers says that when one detaches himself from all determinant knowledge of being, one enters an indeterminate knowledge of being and can determine to be himself in that indeterminate knowledge of being. I think, if I got that said right, that this argues that poetry *does* make something happen, it makes it happen through the poet because of this ability to inhabit the realm of his imagination and being.

This making of the self, the poem, to share with the reader can be aligned with the double movement we discussed earlier, too. This is one of the curious things about "Strip," where you talk about the Möbius strip as a metaphor for this movement: "he // finds himself / turning // back into himself." Lacan and others have used the metaphor to describe the psychological action of the self, which loses itself among those wandering meanings we discussed earlier in order finally to find itself. The thing becomes both an impenetrable knot and a margin between consciousness/unconsciousness and meaning/image. How do all these things we've talked about today—margins, exchanges, crossings over, ambivalences, paces—contribute to a construction of the self?

It's a fair question, but one I haven't thought through in exactly those terms before. I know that I'm not interested in constructing a mask for myself as Yeats did. What I admire rather is how Yeats in the end, and more particularly Stevens in the end, came back down to themselves from self-theorizing altitudes. I suppose that all the fictionalizing is an attempt to imagine himself into other lives so that he can work off some of his own anxieties, tensions. So I don't think of the Möbius strip as a knot, I think of it as the self and other, the two surfaces, reverse and obverse of the same life that does not add up to zero as long as one can see both sides of it. Isn't it Freud, or perhaps a commentator, who says that the ability to live with life's ambiguities is the mark of a mature spirit?

A kind of "Negative Capability"?

I suppose it is, I don't know. I think of it more as an access, a way of returning to the world. Perhaps I've talked myself into a clarity about this today: the poet writes himself down into in order to write himself through, perhaps to some new realm of being which doesn't transcend the old, but gives him more access to what he has always inhabited and will inhabit. In that sense he is changed and so contributes to tipping the balance of the planet, however so slightly. Marianne Moore says in the poem "In Distrust of Merits," something like "Hate-hardened heart, how can I stop the war until I stop the war that is in myself." In that sense, I think the poet can bring himself through to be a survivor of margins, to inhabit the edges of his own existence. With his earned words he has performed a kind of act—to make the poem of the world more accessible to the reader, and so, change the day. Thoreau says somewhere that to affect the quality of the day is the highest of the arts. That seems to me to speak for any art and to be the implicit aim of any poem.

Chances of Survival
Interview by Rachel Berghash, 1988

*In your poem "First Lesson" you say to your daughter: "lie back and
the sea will hold you." I sense here a faith in something beyond oneself.
You wrote this poem thirty years ago and it seems to me from later
poems that you still hold to this view.*

I certainly have a sense of something sustaining beyond one-
self; that there is something out there, whether it's the sea, or
capital *n* Nature, or capital something else. But I think, ratio-
nally, I am both attracted to and skeptical about that possibility.

*In your poem "Sable Island" you say that "No / matter what new
disasters to come, you must shape / your course into the breakers as
though / it were the whole world." There's an art to surviving. What
is it?*

I think survival is at stake for all of us all the time. It always
has been individually, and now it has become demonstrably an
issue that concerns all of us. It's become a universal issue for
the planet. Wherever we are we "have no choice of refuge
left," and we have to think "as though / it were the whole
world"—to quote from "Sable Island." Not that it's a new
feeling that I'm first to express; it's as old as John Donne's "no
man is an island, . . . every man is a piece of the continent, a
part of the main." But I strongly feel that every poem, every
work of art, everything that is well done, well made, well said,

From *The American Poetry Review* 18, no. 3 (May/June 1989): 37–39.

generously given, adds to our chances of survival by making the world and our lives more habitable.

Will this be a stage of flourishing rather than surviving? I see surviving as a first stage, and flourishing as a stage beyond it.

Sure, I think so. I think that my poem "Saying It" reaches toward something like that, in "trying / to say the joy," which is certainly the flourishing or flowering aspect of one's life. I do agree with that very much, as possibility.

I'm interested in your poem "To Chekhov," where you tell him: ". . . you / will be there, waiting, / to tell me where I've been." How do you identify with Chekhov, and what did you discover when you read him?

I can't remember when I first read him, but I do return to him over and over again. One of the remarkable things about a book, whether it's a book of short stories or a book of poems or whatever book it may be, is that it is there for you to go back to over and over again. And I find myself, as many people do, becoming more and more of a re-reader. Not because I've read everything that's brave and beautiful and new, or brave and beautiful and old, but because I want the reassurance of the book being there to resustain me, reinvigorate me, literally offer me a kind of recreation by its very being. And I think that Chekhov particularly—though I like a great number of the Russian writers—seems to get to the essence of human experience marvelously rapidly, with total illusion of casualness, in story after story after story. The variety of experience in those stories is as great as anything I can think of. I know that some people feel that his stories tend to be depressive. I don't feel that, perhaps because I in some senses have a kind of dark view of the world myself. I was very serious in printing, as a headnote to the poem, for some reason I don't now remember, and probably don't want to remember, that there was a November before I wrote that poem when I realized I could not read anybody but Chekhov. I tried to read other writers I had read before, and no one seemed to interest me as much.

Is reading him also helpful in practical terms?

Sure, I go back to saying what I strongly feel: that any good writing makes the world more habitable; and *that* can be, as you said a moment ago, at the level of survival, or at the level of flourishing.

Do you see art as instructive?

I think implicitly it is. I certainly do not consider it to be merely ornamental, but I don't think it's explicitly instructive, or wants to be so. If it is occasionally explicit, as in my poem "First Lesson," it is for me far more metaphorical than literal. There the instruction resonates with all the hopes that one might have for a young daughter and it involves a good deal of fiction as well. I myself was not teaching her to swim. I was watching a young woman, perhaps eighteen or twenty years old, teach her to swim in a village swimming program, in a little town in Vermont one summer, and I noticed the instructress's hand cupping my daughter's head. I realized then how often I had done that, whether when holding her as a baby or putting her up on my shoulder. Obviously such head-holding may be part of making love, and I realized how she was moving toward that age. The fiction is between a father and daughter, the instruction is explicit, but metaphorical. If there is instruction in art, it is best when implicit, perhaps even subliminal, I would say.

Will the poet hope that his/her art will be instructive even if the original intention is not so?

Possibly, sure. A woman who had been a nun, remarkably enough, told me about ten years ago that she had been swept by the currents off Jones Beach beyond the lifeguards, and as she lay there trying to recover herself, she said to herself a part of my poem over and over again: "lie back and the sea will hold you." I was just immensely touched by that.

I can see that. I am struck by that poem because it has a religious note to it. And the fact that a nun was saved remembering it does not surprise me at all.

She might have found better prayers to guide her, but I'm glad she remembered the poem too.

You have been living in close proximity to nature. Does nature have a healing function for you?

It does. But I don't think I can or want to define that in programmatic terms. I don't think I'm a programmatic person in any way. If I'm concerned about nature I'm concerned with the immediacy of it, and in its own restorative powers.

In your poem "The Gate" you say ". . . returned / from this field's large history / into the world of small wars." Does nature restore the injuries inflicted on us when we live in the world?

I do think it does, or it does for me. It did for John Muir. It did for Thoreau. It did for Melville. I speak in another breath when I speak of them, but I'm glad to be a part of that company.

You've spent most of your life in Maine, and your family has been living in the same house for five generations. What are the implications of being so rooted?

My mother's family has been here in this town since 1797. I suppose that I am fundamentally Thoreauvian in that rooted instinct, even as Thoreau said he had travelled much in Concord. I'm not a very good traveller. I like to know every aspect of my locality, wherever it is. When I lived in New York for a year I would often take the subway from Times Square up to Columbia University. And it bothered me very much that even though I followed the green or red lights (whichever they were then) to get the subway from Times Square to the university, it seemed to me when I sat in the subway that it took off backwards, because I thought I was facing north. I was making a wrong turn in my head. And I was even so curious as to take a compass with me once to find out where I was making that wrong turn in my head. Of course there was too much metal underground and I couldn't find where true north was anyway. I tell this only as an indication of how surely I like to know where I am. Only when I in some sense feel that I know where I am, am I able to look down into as well as to look out toward.

Socrates didn't travel at all; he stayed in Athens all his life.

We're talking pretty big names now.

I would like for you to tell us more about what it's like to be rooted.

I'm serious when I say in my poem "Before Sleep" that almost all my mother's ancestors—my grandparents, great-grandparents, great-great, and so on—are buried in the cemetery here. In the November of the year I often go and look at their graves and see their names and the years carved on them. It gives me a very pleasant and not at all morbid sense of the relations, the relationships, that one has with a place. Here, the cemetery gives as good a view of the harbor as one can imagine, and one can think of the women in the family watching out for their husbands' ships to come in. That's an easy association to make. And the fact that the harbor looks now exactly as it did topographically when they were here more than a hundred years ago pleases me immensely. It gives me a deeper insight, literally, into the harbor and whatever my own resonances with my ancestors' experiences may be. I don't like in the casual sense "to make a thing" of it. I do make poems of it, but it seems to me that nobody should, or wants to make the claim, "I was here first, you were here second" or whatever; that's straight out of the Daughters of the American Revolution, and it is terrible. But the sense of rootedness and place is for me a way of feeling—to go back to what you said may be the religious aspect of my work—the holiness of a place.

You probably get to know it better each time; it's like going back to Chekhov.

Absolutely. The title of my recent book is *Relations: Selected Poems 1950–1985*. I have no worry at all about the fact that I've dealt with some of the same subjects over and over in, I hope, varying perspectives, various lights if you will, to transfer the metaphor into painting. Cézanne—to speak in a different breath again—painted "Mont Sainte-Victoire" any number of times, and each of those paintings is different, and each of them casts light on the other.

Is there an evolution in your view in regard to the place?

I think so, but I don't know what it is. I can't name it outside the way the poems themselves try to come to terms with it, whatever it is. It isn't a conscious reaching for evolution on my part. Every poem is in itself separate. I think I've only once written a poem to be part of a book, an explicit part of a particular book. But I've always had more poems, most previously printed in journals, than I needed for a book; so that I've selected in almost every book those poems which seemed to center around some particular concern that was there for me to understand only after I'd written the majority of the poems, and was able to look at them all as a prospective book. I feel very much that way about *Relations*. I could have selected other poems, most of them I suppose lesser poems, and arrived at a considerably different book; so that the poems that I have selected in this so to speak big book, as compared to the individual books, make a larger kind of gestalt. If I pull one poem out the whole book changes, or if I add another the whole book changes, not very much, but in ways at least discernible to me.

Could you talk about the reason behind entitling your book Relations?

I mean relations in all senses. In the sense of the interrelation-ship of poem with poem, and the sequence of a given book's poems with the sequence of another book's poems. I mean relations in the sense of relating a story, an implied narrative, as in the poem "To Chekhov" or any number of the other poems. But I also mean it most of all in terms of the relations that one has humanly to his people and his place, as those circles, even in the perhaps very circumscribed realm in which I live, represent concentric rings moving out, becoming, I hope, ever wider. I don't think of myself as a localist in the sense of being provincial, in saying that this is the way it is in *this* place. I think this is the way it is with being human in most places, in all places, at least within a certain frame of time and of geography. Obviously it isn't the same in Sardinia or Zanzi-bar, and I have, with Thoreau, been disinclined "to count the cats in Zanzibar," so I can't tell about that.

Of course if you probe into the nature of one place you are going to have a universal application.

That is my hope and certainly that has become, as I've become aware of it, part of my aesthetic. I don't think that I'm a Maine, M-A-I-N-E poet, any more than Fairfield Porter is a Maine, M-A-I-N-E painter.

My impression from reading your poetry is that you are not. Your poems have a universal ring to them. The issues are certainly univer-sal. In your later poems you have been more determined to probe into the nature of being, which I see as part of the evolution in your work. Is there anything else that accounts for that evolution, except for going back and looking at what is it to be?

No, I agree with you. I think that that is probably what you are calling the evolutionary process involves for me now—large and small questions about the meaning of being. What does it mean to be able to ask what does it mean to be? I think I'm inherently fascinated by that kind of basically philosophical question, although I find philosophy very difficult to read and am very poor at reading it. Certain images from philosophers like Jaspers and Husserl strike me, and I've made use of them in various poems. Where I've made use of them I hope I've paid my debt to them, and I hope at the same time that what I've done with them has become my own. They have simply been catalytic agents, not so much for what I've thought, but more for how I've felt.

In a good number of your later poems you talk about the meaning of nothing. You say that it is "an acute presence of absence," as against the "raw beauty of being." When I read this I understood it as a way of being which is egoless, and therefore more integrated with oneself and the world.

It does seem to me that ego can become part of a kind of universal ego. Not that the self is submerging its ego to become part of that whole, but that the presence of the ego in the self can become part of a larger "raw beauty of being," to pick up the line you just quoted. I am tempted to extend this and say that such integration strengthens the so-to-speak ego of the whole. That is a fair enough extension of let's say psychoanalytic theory, although I don't often think in terms of the theory. It is much more an intuitive sense that I have. I think it's Masefield who says in a poem, maybe it's in "Dauber," "The days that make us happy make us wise." That comes back to your sense of there being something beyond survival, something in the fruition of one's feeling, the flowering that is itself a wisdom which is sustaining. And its name is joy.

Is joy something you attain easily or with difficulty?

I don't think that one can search for joy, or buy joy, or take out a map and draw a straight line toward joy. I think that there is a great deal of serendipity involved. It often happens when one least expects it. Not necessarily when one least expects it, but not necessarily when one is looking for it. A poem of mine called "How to See Deer" says that if you go out looking for deer you do not see deer. In his story "The Bear" Faulkner uses that point when he writes about the young boy going out into deep woods in the deep South trying to search for an almost mythical bear. But he doesn't see the bear until he casts away his gun and puts away his compass. I saw a deer last night not half a mile from where we are sitting now in your house. It might have come down from the reservoir at the top of the peninsula and run over your lawn for all I know; but for me the deer was a joy to which one could make oneself available as one makes oneself available to the possibility of a poem. If you think about nothing but boats, or if you think about nothing but houses, or if you think about nothing but (in a man's case) women, or (in a woman's case) perhaps men, it's pretty hard to arrive at the kind of joy that you imagine you are searching for.

I had a teacher, Dr. P. G. McLean, a psychiatrist and philosopher, who said that the aim of life is to live and die without regret, and that living and dying with joy is one kind of regret-free living and dying. It seems to me that joy is hard to attain.

Yes it does seem so to me. I think that there is a sense where each of us may have a certain background—yours may be Old Testament and mine may be New England Puritan, but I think they are conjoined very deeply beyond any such distinction— which tends us toward a view of life that is perhaps similar. And even Freud's was similar in that sense that he did not expect one to be universally healthy after a course of psycho-analysis. But I think we are talking about tapping into our roots—quite beyond any particular psychoanalytic theory. Even as Jung believed there was a universal unconscious, not merely a subconscious, to which we would all be open if we could.

I think that there is a distinction between joy and happiness. One of the ways to feel joy is to transcend circumstances. Whereas to be happy you would have to have had an upbringing under pretty lucky circum-stances, and that's uncommon.

And to be continually happy is impossible.

I am reminded of your poem "Adding it Up," where you say: "I'm Puritan to the bone, down to / the marrow and then some: / if I'm not sorry I worry, / if I can't worry I count." Could you tell us more about the kind of impositions or self-impositions that Puritanism entails?

I come literally from families that were basically Puritan on both sides, my father's and my mother's. I was brought up in rather strict Victorian conventions to the extent that I was in many ways inhibited early on in ways that I tried to work out, as many boys do, through sports, and so on. It wasn't until I was perhaps in my thirties that I felt fundamentally (no, I don't suppose ever fundamentally), *mostly* free of those inhibitions, those imposed elements of superego.

In your poem "Watch" you say: "There is no end to the lies / we devise to live by . . ." and in your poem "Not to Tell Lies" you say: ". . . he has gathered himself / in order not / to tell lies." Is this determination part of getting older?

I think that only after you've grown well beyond your majority of twenty-one do you begin to see how many lies you have at various times in your life devised for yourself. So I suppose you are right that it is a matter of age, although not necessarily a matter of becoming wiser with age, unless there is some wisdom in trying not to tell lies. But that doesn't mean for me, in these poems or in any art, not telling fictions, because I think that the fictions can be truer than true. Some of the images in both the poems you mentioned, particularly in "Not to Tell Lies," although they derive from my so-to-speak auto-biographical experiences, are fictions. The images are not fictionalized in the sense that I merely transpose purple to green or uncle to aunt. The fictions of poetry are at their best, as Wallace Stevens very well knew, acts of imagination, and they come from a much deeper source then merely transposing one fact from another in order to avoid a libel suit.

In your poem "Eaton's Boatyard" you say: "to forget for good / all the old year's losses, / save for / what needs be retrieved." It's a wonderful piece of teaching. Are the losses that need to be retrieved in life or in art, or in both?

I'd like to correct your question. You said "that need *to be* retrieved," and although the poem is full of infinitives there isn't one in that particular place. My slight yearning is to feel that whatever is to be retrieved has some life of its own that *wants* to be retrieved; that the word, like the part that is being searched for in the boatyard, almost wants at a certain point to make itself available to the poet, if he is only open enough to let it come at him. That's only answering a very small part of your question, because I do mean that losses must be to a certain extent forgotten if one is to move beyond them. But again the poem says: "to forget for good / all the old year's losses . . . ," and I'd emphasize that "for good" is out there in an end of a line where it means to me (in the prosody of this particular poem) that forgetting "for good" is different than forgetting "for bad" reasons. Certain things need be forgotten, if you will, both in a poem and obviously in our lives if we are to get on with what we must write, or what we must do, or how we must live. But I think that nothing is ever totally forgotten. We only push some things deeper than others, and they too may present themselves, or we may be able to retrieve them when we need them.

I think of retrieving in the sense of restoring or making reparation.

Yes. I think that what you are calling reparation is a way of redeeming whatever relationship is involved, whether it's a relationship of a boatbuilder with his wood, or whether it's a relationship of a poet with a bad line in a poem that he can redeem somehow, not by forgetting that it is bad but bringing variants or revisions back into consciousness by way of a different route of some sort. What that route is depends on the wrong turn the line originally took.

And I am thinking in terms of an interpersonal relationship where we have damaged someone and we are making reparation.

Yes, of course. Although that seems to me to be in some way at a different level psychologically as well as morally, or sociomorally. It can sometimes be merely a matter of good manners, or it can be of large social morality. I have to think of it on both a larger and smaller scale of life and of art.

I am talking about genuine making reparation that would be creative. In physiology it would be the process in which a broken bone is healed.

I understand. The word reparation isn't very much in my vocabulary. Obviously for some damages there can be no reparation.

Right. Where the thing is dead. In that case one can make vicarious reparation, in a relationship or in art perhaps. Correct me if I am wrong: you might write a bad poem and you can't do anything about it. And the next thing you do is write a good poem.

But I don't think that happens consciously, the way one can be conscious about the injustice one has done to someone else, and consciously try to do something about it. If I write a poem that I soon feel is bad, I don't go out on a damage control mission to write a next poem in order to repair the first. I have to think otherwise about it. I have to try to forget the bad for good. And, in a different sense, try to make good on what comes next.

Relations

Interview by Stephen Dunn, 1985

This interview took place off and on during the afternoon and eve-
ning of December 5, 1985, in Philip and Margaret Booth's house in
Castine, Maine, a small coastal town where Booth's ancestors have
lived since 1797, and where—since he shifted from full-time to half-
time teaching at Syracuse University some ten years ago—he lives
eight months of the year.

I had thought about doing an interview with him because his poems
over recent years have become so strong and deep, but I especially
wanted to do it after—at my request—he sent me his new manuscript
Relations: Selected Poems 1950–1985, *which was published by*
Viking/Penguin *in May, 1986, and contains selections from his six*
previous books. Moreover, it seemed important to do the interview in
Castine, rather than, say, Syracuse, which was more convenient for
me to get to. Castine is more than just home to Booth. As our walks
around town substantiated, it is where many of his "relations" are,
both in terms of people and place. It is the wellspring of much of his
work, though his poetry is never regional in the narrow sense.

We talked in his upstairs study, in a wing of the large ancestral
house the Booths have remodeled to live in since their three grown
daughters have moved away.

ια

The epigraph from Thoreau at the beginning of the new book, "Not
until we are lost do we begin to find ourselves and realize where we

From *New England Review* 9, no. 2 (Winter 1986): 134–58. Reprinted
by permission of *NER* and Stephen Dunn.

are in the infinite extent of our relations," seems crucial to your work, and Thoreau certainly seems to hover over the book. I wonder if you would talk about the importance of Thoreau to you and your work, and maybe why you seized upon that quote of his.

Sure. I must say that I think of myself, internally, as being Thoreauvian in some ways. I think I am something of an odd stick, I think I am fundamentally a loner, although I have better protective coloration in social contexts than Thoreau did. I don't mean that I think of myself as being Thoreauvian in yearning for wilderness as such, or wanting to go camping on Walden Pond permanently. It was just chance that in 1954 I moved to Lincoln, Massachusetts, very near Walden, about the time that I got started writing seriously.

I still have here the copy of *Walden* that I had in school, the Modern Library edition, and I had forgotten until this moment that as a junior in school I wrote what you can see: the printed hardcover reads "*Walden* / Thoreau," and I added under *Walden* "is obviously insane" [*laughter*]. So clearly my sense of Thoreau was passionate from the first, if negative.

I am wondering if there was any particular time when your life kind of caught up to the quote, especially the first part of it, "Not until we are lost," or have you lived with that notion before or all along?

No, I certainly have not lived with it all along. The first poem in the book is called "Adam" and was one of the first poems I'd written after having moved to Massachusetts down from New Hampshire and from here [in Maine]. During the first year of that move my mother died in a mental hospital; her death there was my own fall out of Eden. When my mother broke, and died, I was soon lost in my own lostness. Within several years after her death it caught up with me very hard, so that I myself got pretty shaky, and by great good fortune went into psychoanalysis as a control, so called, of a young medical doctor who herself was going through training in the Boston Psychoanalytic Institute. It turned out to be a classic Freudian analysis, five days a week. . . .

Five days a week. Truly serious analysis . . .

For three and a half years. I don't mean now to pull up my shirt like President Johnson and show an appendectomy scar which looks like Vietnam [*laughing*]. That's thirty years behind me now, but there isn't any question but that I was lost, in Thoreau's sense. My own sense of being lost, and *surviving*, gets said in "The Line," which was, I think, as early as *The Islanders*.

I didn't know you were going to start on this, yet I've just been reading Albert Gelpi's book about Emily Dickinson, and right at the beginning of it, he talks about Thoreau speaking of a man's birth as "a sundering of things, as if" (now Gelpi is quoting Thoreau) " 'we had been thrust up through into nature like a wedge.' " And Gelpi goes on to say the life process is a "healing of raw wounds, knitting the individual to his foreign environs." It seems to me that need to heal happens even for those of us who are most rooted.

Were you consciously cultivating your roots by moving your life toward Maine, living on terms that were more your own?

Well, yes, living on terms that were more my own. But I might shift the metaphor: I think now it was a matter of mooring myself in a known harbor, in order to sail out from it.

Let me try to get back to what you asked at first, back to the epigraph. Finding in losing seems to me to be the chief paradox of Christianity. I'm not a member of any church, but I think that it is true in a large emotional way for those of us brought up in whatever Western tradition that Thoreau is right: "Not until we are lost do we begin to find ourselves." Frost's poem "Directive" is made of that paradox. "And if you're lost enough to find yourself . . . ," Frost says.

Well, in some sense, I've always known where I was, physically, and I've always been certain of where my roots were. But only more recently have I become more aware of Thoreau's sense of "the infinite extent of our relations." It's clear to me now that I've been saving that quotation, subconsciously perhaps, waiting for the time when it would be right, and I think I knew it was going to be right when I had a book that could be called *Relations*.

The word "relations" instead of, say, "relationships," I'm sure, pleases you in its resonances. The word embraces relationships, of course, but I'm sure you wanted the fullest range of connotation from that word. . . .

Yes, I mostly want that. From as far back as teaching Freshman English at Wellesley, I've talked about relationships. And have said that "nothing exists in isolation." Only now, since I've written so much about "nothing" in *Before Sleep,* do I also see that that makes a different kind of statement. Nothing *does* exist in isolation. Total isolation *is* nothing. But this side of nothing everything exists in relation.

Do you mean that also in the sense of your poetics, the way a poem and words and lines exist in relation to other lines and words, how the lines and words in relation to each other compel you to find limits, to keep limits?

Yes, that too. I've just finished writing a piece for a Festschrift that made me look back at Richard Wilbur's essay in *Mid-Century American Poets,* which is about that very point. And I was thinking how much, *just* when I began to write, I was impressed that Wilbur *had* a theory of limits. I'm sure that appealed to my Puritan background, my Puritan, I guess, psyche. On the shore of a Walden Pond watching whatever concentric rings might spread from a pebble, rather than running around the pond, to see how many times I could do it [*laughter*] in fifty minutes. Limits make sense to me in what you're calling poetics. Thoreau says somewhere, "Do nothing against your genius." Clearly he means that last word not in terms of anything as foolish as a high I.Q. or Army General Intelligence Test, but against what you were given in your genes . . . .

It seems to me that in the early poems in Relations *your prosody is more or less inherited. But as we progress through that book we see you more and more finding a prosody, a syntax, that is peculiarly yours.*

I hope that's so.

And even dramatically so in the new poems.

It's unquestionably true that I inherited prosody of the fifties, so to speak; the prosody, the syntax, the metaphysics, that whole inclination which seemed to me immensely modern because [*laughter*] it simply coincided with my trying to come of age. I've intuitively moved toward a prosody that is both more individual and more open. My prosody now is far from his, but I know I tried early to learn from people like Wilbur. I've never given up admiring how Wilbur has held to his own territory. But more and more I've learned from poets to the left of me, if you will, rather than the more major poets that everybody has learned from.

You seem to be one of the poets, rare in American literary history, who has pushed his work forward in his fifties, have done in fact your best work during that time and continue to do so now, during this year, your sixtieth. It seems to be remarkable. I can think of maybe Williams, Penn Warren, not too many have done that. I'm not sure exactly what I want to ask you, but it's something perhaps as simple [laughter] *as "How have you done it?" But maybe even more pointedly, what were the things you had to overcome, if you could name some, to keep the work going? Was it something to do with how your career has evolved, or perhaps the way you've chosen to live your life, that is to say not as a public poet? You can plug into these questions any way you want.*

[*laughing*] Well, it's either all of the above or none of the above. But I do think it's all of them. I think I learned things from teaching Stevens at Syracuse that I didn't know I needed. I think I learned something about trying to get at ideas. In "Notes toward a Supreme Fiction," you remember that Stevens says, "It Must Be Abstract. It Must Give Pleasure. It Must

129

Change." I think what happened was that I gave up, not consciously, some of the sense that "it must give pleasure" in favor of the possibilities that it must be *more* abstract than my early poems, or that it must abstract certain elements from the nature of those poems. And certainly it must change, it must change with change, whatever it is. What is "it"? Well, for Stevens, the supreme fiction, and just as I'm now analyzing my own sense of Stevens' very precise assertions, it seems to me too that my poems have in some strange way become more fictional, even as they appear to be more autobiographical.

Talk about that.

I think I'll have to come back to it, I'm not sure that I can. I'd like to pick up on what you said a minute ago. You said something about not being a public poet, is that right?

Yes. I was wondering about what seems to be a very conscious choice of yours over the last many years not to do readings, to come back home to Castine, to more or less stay here and work.

How much of it owes to forces in me that I know nothing about, I'm not sure; but there certainly was some conscious choice in it. I might take reading up again I suppose, but I think probably not. I haven't read since I read at Syracuse with George Elliott, Donald Justice, W. D. Snodgrass, for Eugene McCarthy, in what must have been '68. I've read for small groups of friends, but not in a public session. I grew to feel some intuitive sense, not any programmatic sense, that a lot of the poets with whom I, in one way or another, grew up, had gotten to repeat themselves more and more because of the adulation that had come to them from public performance. Having written poem x, poet M tended to rewrite the poem as x-subscript one, x-subscript two, over and over. In all sorts of guises. And maybe it was just a Puritan fear of doing as little that drove me to take another tack. I've never thought that I read particularly well. I know how much reading always took out of me: thinking about it in advance, worrying about it, so that I found myself pushing poems away in favor of thinking about the reading. What's happened is, I think, that I've written a good number of poems that would never have gotten written if I'd thought about them as poems in any way to be "published." If I'd thought about them on *any* terms but their own.

There are terms that keep on cropping up in the poems which seem related to the quest of "finding the extent of our relations"—a word like "try," for example, and another would be "almost." One of the things that makes the poems so credible to me as reader is the sense that the poems offer no certainties and a good part of their authority comes from how well the voice in the poems embraces uncertainty. The words testify to a groping of the most fundamental sort. I think what's happening in the new poems is that the syntax is also registering that; this intellectual groping of yours is so emotionally grounded, and the syntax evidences this.

I'm glad you feel that. Again that's a pretty intuitive thing. Ten days ago Margaret and I went to the Renoir show in Boston. And after seeing Renoir, who is an attractive painter, but not a terribly interesting one, I went to the Impressionists Room where I hadn't been in maybe twenty years to show Margaret the big Gauguin which says up in the corner "Where did we come from? Where are we? Where are we going?" I just now think Gauguin's questions corroborate what you're saying; a searching not so much for absolute certainty as for a way through. A searching that can be stated pretty simply in a phrase Josephine Miles used recently for a title, but which I've also been using for years: "coming to terms." Coming to terms with whatever experience is involved. I consciously in *Relations* put the poem "Adam" first because in that poem Adam is still partially prelapsarian, he has not entirely fallen out of Eden, and he is simply the poet as namer, the nominalist: "that was the name thereof," says Genesis. Well, the names were there once he said them; they were sure, they were perfect. But part of the fall into consciousness is being conscious of how we know what we know, a kind of epistemological or psychoanalytic procedure. And as my own consciousness has increased— perhaps a kind of *felix culpa*—from teaching poets like Stevens, from early joy in Elizabeth Bishop, it seems to me I've moved more and more away from nominalism to a broader kind of "coming to terms" that you very generously say involves matters syntactical and rhythmical.

Would you add George Oppen to that list of influences? He has in one of his poems lines that say "possible / to use / words, provided one treat them / as enemies," which when I read I thought of you immediately. You seem to want to confront words, get everything out of them, and in your later work especially much of the tension seems to come from a resistance to the conventional meanings of words. Does that make sense to you?

Yes, I think I know what George means, but I don't think of words as enemies in any sense. I think there is a resistance that is more like the resistance of sailing to windward and having to tack by necessity as the wind changes slightly. There is a kind of prosody, a more conventional prosody, which allows one to sail with beautiful freedoms within a closed course. As, paradoxically enough, in the famous line from Williams: "The yachts / contend in a sea which the land partly encloses." If you want to run triangular courses and exhibit your skills competitively, that's one way to sail; it's also one way to write poems. But if you're not writing an entirely closed poem or if your inclination is not to *impose* limits, but to stretch the limits of your own ability, to proceed with them offshore, perhaps in fog [*laughter*], with no particular course in mind, because the weather feels right to be out in, or . . .

That's a philosophical position, isn't it, as much as it is a compositional one?

Sure, it isn't simply compositional. Because what is unknown *must* be confronted. In that what is most unknown, death, cannot be avoided, everything else en route to death must be confronted. Confronted even if to be backed away from, but not to be avoided.

You have a poem in Available Light *called "Ways" in which you posit different scenarios about death, or ways in which one might die. It's a poem I like, though when I read the poems in* Before Sleep *it seems a slight poem by comparison. In* Before Sleep *the ways in which you confront your own mortality, and the mortality of others—Lowell, Arendt, Donald Dike—takes on a depth and resonance that may not have been there before in your work.*

Oh, I think it certainly wasn't there before. It wasn't that I wasn't trying to get toward it, but I didn't know what it was. In the *Letter from a Distant Land* poems, there's a poem called "Storm in Formal Garden," which is an attempt to confront my mother's illness and to "rake" my own way through the weeds that were clogging that rake. I had the distinction, not uncommon with first books about that time, of having John Simon pan me . . .

Oh God . . . .

[*Laughter*] . . . egregiously, and he picked on that poem particularly as a sentimental occasion hardly worthy of his scorn. Maybe he was right to some extent, but I included the poem back into *Relations,* as it was not included in *Margins* [Booth's previous Selected] because it did seem to me to be a poem that's predictive in some way of what might happen to the persona of these poems, as the book moves on. And that predictive confrontation, that trying "to come to terms," has to do with what you just said about the poems in *Before Sleep,* it may have to do with my giving up something of Stevens' directive, that "it must give pleasure."

I wonder if you'd talk a little more about that, since "pleasure" is a problematical word in that the poems now give a different kind of pleasure. Could you make a distinction between the kind of pleasure you were vouchsafing and . . .

Well, I think that I thought a poem as limited as "Vermont: Indian Summer," very early on, a pure lyric to the season, was a poem of "pleasure." It pleasures my ear still in some way. But I also think—I've long thought—that Auden was fundamentally wrong in saying in his elegy for Yeats that "poetry makes nothing happen: it survives / In the valley of its saying where executives / Would never want to tamper." I don't think it merely survives in the valley of its own saying, never mind executives; it seems to me that a good poem makes the world more habitable, and it gives, therefore, a different kind of pleasure: it stretches not toward mere pleasure, but toward joy. I cannot believe that a good poem does not have, if different in degree, at least some of the effect that for me Beethoven's Ninth Symphony does. It may start out, as much music does, with a kind of consolation for suffering, but the Ninth Symphony comes to joy, quite beyond Schiller's lyrics. I think that a poem can be full of joy—no, that isn't true—a poem can *reach toward* joy and sometimes touch joy and touch in others, the reader, the joy of being so true to human experience that however painful it may seem, it is finally sustaining.

One of the concerns that keeps recurring in your later poems is not just what it's like to be alive, but what it feels *like to be alive. I've of course had that feeling with the best of poems, that feeling of assent to someone else's rightness, which is also your own.*

I'd go back to George Oppen and say certain poems of his certainly give me that feeling. Nobody needed to tell me how to feel about them; their emotion inheres. Another poet who deeply struck me was Jeffers. I was quite young, years before writing was in me, but I'm sure that his example of staying to his own emotional territory and mining it deeply must have had some effect on me. I don't really like most of the long dramatic poems, but I can remember long later reading the *Hungerfield* poems and weeping as I read them. I read the book through in one night. And I felt much the same way about *The Beginning and the End.* A lot of those shorter poems seemed to me to hold nothing back of what in Jeffers was anger, bitterness, but never anything as cheap as resentment. And he got it said.

Somehow this is all adding up to, I'm not sure exactly, but let's call it morality in poetry. Would you venture . . .

Probably not [*laughter*].

. . . what the poet's moral obligation is, if he or she has one at all. Stevens says something like "It's to register the right sensation."

I believe it's a lot more than that. [*Long pause.*] Well, I suppose I don't know. I *certainly* don't know. But I suppose I tried to tell myself something of that in the poem which began *Before Sleep*, "Not to Tell Lies." Which, though it puts it negatively, says something about my instinctive response to falsifying. . . . We're subjected to so much lying from high places, we're bombarded by falsehood on the television; we're so emotionally assaulted by all of this, we so lightly lie to ourselves in our lesser and sometimes in our deeper relations, including our relations with ourselves, that there is a tremendous need for the poet to know that he or she is not—through whatever abstracting or fictionalizing—telling lies. If that has something to do with the morality of the art, so be it. Sure it does. Because it seems to me that all art that aspires to art, and does not tell lies, is essentially moral.

What do you think the role of craft is in this? Because it could be anybody's wish not to tell lies, of course, and we might not pay much attention. There seems to be something in how one goes about achieving "not to tell lies" in one's art that is special and differentiating.

Well, I think those poets among us who want extremely structured poems that move by comparatively formal measures through the resonances of skillfully heard rhymes and such could argue their case very well on that ground, and I don't want to argue for them. I think, though, that I've come to a different sense of wanting to let more *in* to the poem, more possibility into the poem. And I found that made possible for me as the structures of my own poems began to find new ways to open themselves, and curved me more to the poems I'm now writing. Trying to make *Relations* whole, I had to think about my changing sense of craft. I had to drop out a good number of poems I in various ways *liked* but didn't much respect. And I had to put early poems back even where they showed limitations much beyond any theory of limits [*laughter*], but were still trying to get toward something that later I may have come closer to. It occurs to me now, since I mentioned "Not to Tell Lies," that I actually wrote another poem of that same title over thirty years ago, about a man and a woman walking in woods, trying to reconcile some difference between them, and trying not to tell lies to themselves. It wasn't much of a poem. But the title must have impressed me once I discovered it since it came back to me years later. And, to follow up on what you said before, about returning to my Maine life, the present "Not to Tell Lies" *is*, after all, about returning to this house and writing in the back bedroom with my ancestors' portraits on the wall, with the rock a doctor brought me back from Amchitka—though those images are fictionalized *in order* not to tell lies.

You mentioned earlier that your poems have become more fictive. That's the real reason, isn't it, to include things in a poem, not necessarily because they happened, but because they will be useful in the larger service of truth? To find those things that will be emblematic of the truth?

Yes, and the poem which most focuses, or which most recently tries to come to terms with that problem, is a poem called "Table." It's in one sense about a bedside table, but it also makes a claim that the man, before going to sleep, accepts things such as *The Portable Chekhov*, and "a photograph of his wife some forty years since," as *they* self-present themselves to him. And that presentation seems to me to involve opening the poem, which is to say opening oneself sufficiently to let the possibilities of the poem enter. And though I still find a great deal of him beyond my comprehension, I think John Ashbery deserves a lot of praise from any of us for having shown, in effect, how much can enter the poem.

At the same time I can't think of anyone who is more antithetical to your way of composing poems. In fact, as I was reading these new poems of yours I was feeling how they make so many other poets I read seem evasive, and Ashbery would certainly be one of those poets.

Sure, that's a judgment that could be made, but I think that nonetheless the aleatory possibilities that John has made realizable in his poems have provided ways for the rest of us to let our own *apparently* random possibilities enter the poems . . . . Once you're past basic anatomy, I think you can learn more from those poets who are unlike you than those who are like you.

At the end of "Table," the last few lines give thanks "to any words that might measure." I didn't count them, but the amount of times that the word "measure" is mentioned in the new poems suggests a preoccupation, not unlike Williams' during his career—his good efforts at finding a measure in free verse. I wonder how you yourself are using that word? It seems, to me, you mean it in at least two ways. Prosodically, of course, and also as a synonym for exactitude. Or are you only thinking of it in terms of prosody?

No, though "Table" involves the idea of a table of measurement, I'm not directly thinking of it in terms of prosody. But I think the poem includes some larger sense of measure. Take the man in Frost's "The Star Splitter" who burned his house down in order to buy a telescope so that he could "satisfy a lifelong curiosity / About our place among the infinities." Frost talks more than once about measuring against the All. This has nothing to do with measuring the azimuth of Halley's Comet. It has something to do with my own inmost being, not my heart, not my mind, but my total self; it has something to do with how a human being measures against all that surrounds him. Against all that he is within himself, against all that exists in relation to him. Whether in overt relationship, or only in implicit relationship.

In how anything singular relates beyond itself I also feel a certain sense of the *un*certainty—we all live in a rather remarkable gestalt in which even the slightest change in any aspect of our lives affects all other aspects.

And you want to measure that?

The lines are: ". . . the other and all / to which he woke beholden: // and this day / meant again to try to give thanks to, if / he could for the life of him join and return / any words that might measure." Well, there are a lot of ifs in there, a lot of conditions. But I do want the poem itself to measure the possibility of access to more than its own being. And that possibility, here, much involves the verb "recalled." The man reaches "to find again in the still life there / an issue of something more than itself, / the more and other that over and over / recalled him." It seems to me that "recalled" works with exactly the kind of ambivalence I want in a word like that.

As always, the poem says it the way you most mean it, right?

Well [*laughing*], I was lucky in this poem. That's one of the few poems I've written in a long time that came as rapidly as it did, perhaps because I did let it in. It only went through ten drafts, say. But think of all the qualifications: "if / he could, for the life of him"— this is an issue of life . . . and death. If life, then death. "If / he could, for the life of him, *join* . . . " [*emphasis in Booth's voice, not on the page*]. Quite aside from the making of the poem, this seems to me to speak the man's urge to be part of the wholeness as well as to retain his individual identity. Perhaps "measure" acknowledges both the gap between oneness and allness and, also, the potential to know what they are. All of this is an aspect of what I admire in George Oppen, just as I admire it in Jeffers, his tremendously immediate sense of his place amidst universals. As his title says, "Of Being Numerous." What does it mean to be part of a great number? What does it mean to belong to that number, to be able to say "help me I am / of that people the grass // blades touch . . ."

The implicit notion that there might be ways of partially answering such questions, where we are in relation to things, in relation to others, seems affirmative to me. Pertinent to this, I was very interested in all the uses you make of the word "nothing" in Before Sleep, *which in another person's hands could have been easily nihilistic, but in yours was not. First of all, there is a curious playfulness in how you use and talk about "nothing." . . .*

Through other voices other than my own the play mostly occurs. Through Noam, for instance. My own voice is mostly more serious.

But I think of it as a kind of play for mortal stakes, that you're getting every possible meaning and nuance out of nothing and nothingness, yet I never have a sense of nihilistic vision behind the poems. What's operative is much more a philosophical probing. . . .

Yeah, I like that as a phrase, I wouldn't have thought of that. No, I don't feel nihilistic at all.

Nor are you an absurdist, even though your poems entertain the notion that the world is absurd. But you never stop there. It all has to do with "relations," I think, that relations (in the broad sense) seem to give you a way to affirm in the face of uncertainties. I'm thinking now how the title poem of the new book ends, "By how / to each other / we're held, we keep / from spinning out / by how to each other / we hold." Those lines which I find so wonderful are, it seems, central to your way of looking at things. Your poems may flirt with absurdity and nihilism, but . . .

I don't think of myself in categories, absurdist or nihilist or anything of the kind. I find it very hard to read philosophy. One of my sons-in-law gave me Jaspers for a Christmas present some ten years ago, a thin little book of Jaspers from which I drew an epigraph for the poem "It Is Being." Everytime I read Jaspers I had to reread the last three pages I'd read in order to get ahead one more page. I don't think easily or well in abstract terms, but that's all an aside to the fact that, indeed, both the poem "Before Sleep" and the poem "Relations" are poems that mean to give thanks back to what in this village sustains me. It is my way of returning words, not programmatically or even consciously as I write the poem, but as they remain after the fact as a kind of thanksgiving. In the way that all good poems extend as well as intend, it seems to me; and I go back to saying that any good poem, any great symphony, any good Coleman Hawkins riff, makes the world more habitable. Because it changes the world. It changes the world slightly in favor of being alive and being human.

I'd like you to read, if you will, the poem "Saying It."

Saying It

Saying it. Trying
to say it. Not
to answer to

logic, but leaving
our very lives open
to how we have

to hear ourselves
say what we mean.
Not merely to

know, all told,
our far neighbors;
or here, beside

us now, the stranger
we sleep next to.
Not to get it said

and be done, but to
say the feeling, its
present shape, to

let words lend it
dimension: to name
the pain to confirm

how it may be borne:
through what in
ourselves we dream

to give voice to,
to find some word for
how we bear our lives.

Daily, as we are daily
wed, we say the world
is a wedding for which,

as we are constantly
finding, the ceremony
has not yet been found.

What wine? What bread?
What language sung?
We wake, at night, to

imagine, and again wake
at dawn to begin: to let
the intervals speak

for themselves, to
listen to how they
feel, to give pause

to what we're about:
to relate ourselves,
over and over; in

time beyond time
to speak some measure
of how we hear the music:

today if ever to
say the joy of trying
to say the joy.

A wonderful poem. One of the things that's striking to me about it, and this is true of several other poems in the new poems, is that you write the poem directly, in language that is the unadorned language of its subject, without looking for correlatives. It's interesting especially because so many of your previous poems, and poems that also work well, choose to speak through place and are metaphorical—exhibit the pleasures of ulteriority. This poem, however, seems to me the apogee of many that speak directly and not only directly but abstractly. And is this a direction for you? Would you like to speak like this in all of your poems if you could get away with it?

I don't think it's either / or. And I don't think it has become a conscious choice for me as a new mode in which to proceed. It seems to me more something that has evolved in the course of these books, in the course of my life, toward risking the kinds of simplicity that are implicit here. But I think it also occurs—you're nice enough to say this is the apogee of it, and it may be—in poems like "A Man in Maine," which proceeds pretty much by the same means, in some ways, involving recurrence, moving by recurrence. It is tactically much the same; the wood is not a metaphor for anything more than itself, and so on. I think what most appeals to me is what you said—that the poem is comparatively abstract. I like that possibility more and more, being able to select *out* what doesn't pertain to the absolute essence of the poem. It seems to me that I've always been a pretty laconic poet, increasingly probably after *The Islanders*. Perhaps a poem like "The Ship" might have been a turn in that direction for me; that's a poem I like quite a good deal. Letting the things speak for themselves, as I just suggested they might in "Table."

A little while ago I said I learned something from Stevens ("it must be abstract"), and I don't think of this as being a Stevens-like poem in any way, but I do think that it both goes directly at its subject—*saying* it—and at the same time it does abstract, which is to say *takes away from* in the sense of paring away everything save what prove to be the essentials. And in that sense I want to mention not in the breath of my poems, but in another breath—when one speaks a large name one has to draw breath: Cézanne. Cézanne is the painter who in many ways most moves me. In the last poem in *Before Sleep* (which draws on an essay by Merleau-Ponty), I have Cézanne speak. Cézanne says of a painting: "I am its consciousness." The consciousness of the "House in the Woods," for instance, which I have freely liberated into being "The House in the Trees" because it seems less pretentious and differently resonant for the purposes of my poem . . . I've known that painting since 1949, since before I was much trying to write. I was at Columbia then and saw the painting and was knocked over by it. In the Modern Museum. Here's [*on the windowsill*] a postcard of another Cézanne, "The House on the River." Jay Meek sent it to me from somewhere. A painting in which very obviously there's a great deal of space around the subject that is centered; and the subject itself is centered in part by the space around it. So a great deal has been abstracted away from the central issue of the painting. And I believe something like that happened in writing "Saying It." I think I'm not talking *about* saying it. I would like to think that in some way I'm the consciousness of the poem's *being the act* of saying it.

Let's say all language is approximate. Metaphorical language is obviously approximate. Yet the kind of abstract language that occurs in this poem seems closer to something, maybe the thing itself. So I'm speculating that when you've gotten your language and statement this clean, that to speak through rocks or stones might seem almost artificial. Of course it's all artifice—what any of us is doing—but artificial in the bad sense of the reader thinking "The poet is writing poetry now, as opposed to speaking to me." This poem is saying it.

I hear that as a possibility. But at the same time I think only certain kinds of subjects admit to the full kind of abstraction that exists in this poem. And as I'm looking at you as we're talking now, there's a bolt on the far windowsill about as long as a small boy's forearm. And that is the bolt of the poem "Bolt," in which I say it is a bolt about as long as a small boy's forearm. [*Laughter.*] And so that is not so much of a metaphor as it is a way of pointing to its size. Of being a preliminary measure of what the poem perhaps finally comes to.

In a sense the same kind of language, the language that makes you think you've only spoken about the thing itself.

"Bolt" is a poem which I want to grant immediately is not as high-risk or high-gain as "Saying It" is—but in that poem the bolt, in effect, is only itself. And the poem makes a point of that. And in so doing, if the bolt is a symbol it is a symbol only of itself. It has abstracted from the bolt things that are *not* possible to say about it. Not without "telling lies."

In "Saying It" I would argue that "the stranger / we sleep next to"—obviously I'm using stranger in some slightly metaphorical sense—is a stranger abstracted from any possibility of narrative action in the poem. And certainly I move the

143

poem into a more familiar realm of abstraction and symbol when I draw on the conventional images: "What wine, what bread," which I acknowledge in a note that I hear as resonating with Stevens' "The American Sublime." Of course "the world / is a wedding" comes from Delmore Schwartz's title, which is itself metaphorical, and comes from the Talmud. I can only say that I've held that in mind since I discovered Delmore's title at about the same time, strangely enough, that I discovered Cézanne. Maybe I ought to go back to the city [*laughter*]—these happened when I was at Columbia. I was so taken by the idea of world as wedding that I added to it what I think is my own thought "for which the ceremony has not yet been found." And I went around to all my teachers, Mark Van Doren and others, and asked where did I learn that? And finally I had to believe that I'd made it up.

You had that line that far back?

Yes, and it didn't occur to me to make use of it until I came to it in this poem. I must have had it very deep in me to be able to draw it up. And the poem is part of the ceremony for me, because the poem is the act that explores the inwardness of one's consciousness back to finding an image of the ceremony not yet found. The line was with me thirty-five years before I wrote the poem. The phrase mediates inward to me and ultimately out to the world—in the sense of a relation that is the ceremony between reader and writer, of sharing the words of the poem in the wedding of how each needs the other.

I know what you're saying about objects like the bolt—almost the way Pound talked about natural objects. If you talk about them accurately they're going to have resonance and symbolic value.

Sufficient in itself.

Yes, there's no sense you're pushing the metaphor at all.

O.K., and I'm sure that I have done that, pushed metaphors at times. I would hope that I pushed them early on in my writing rather than later on. I find that a lot of poets whom I otherwise like seem to me too metaphorical. There's no need to name them, but here I think in "Saying It" the poem moves, not by, as you said, extending the metaphor, but by trying to sustain the very music of the poem. And making the way the poem moves an expression of, analogic to, but an expression of, the process of finding the word.

That seems to me what happens in almost all of the new poems, that the way of saying them is part of the subject matter of the poem. A high achievement, I think.

Well, when I was a kid, about thirteen or fourteen, partially growing up here and partially in Hanover, I used to sneak into the Dartmouth College spring houseparty dances. I'd sneak into the top floor of the gym at four in the afternoon and hide under the bandstand until I got kicked out about nine-thirty at night. I listened close-in to Jimmy Dorsey, Jimmy Lunceford, Louis Armstrong, a lot of them. They had two bands playing opposite sets, as they did in the big dancehalls in Harlem. One wonderful time after I got kicked out and went downstairs, there was a fine musician named Sy Oliver who was down there picking out on the piano, writing, actually writing, what has always been one of my favorite songs as metaphor for what we're talking about: "T'aint what you do, it's the way what you do it. Ain't what you say, it's the way what you say it."

That's a far way back from "Saying It," but I totally remember hearing him hum that, pick out the notes, and *say it.* Who knows what influences a poet? I don't suppose the poem bears directly on Sy Oliver. I don't know nearly as much about jazz as Hayden Carruth and some other poets do, but I feel very strongly about the way rhythms inhere in certain kinds of language, how they inhere in ways that make it possible for the poem to move, and thus move the reader.

Are recurrences a major way to insist on one's rhythms in an abstract poem?

I don't know. I suppose probably. As you've probably noticed, I've learned to move the recurrences *around* in their positions in lines, and in stanzas or strophes, particularly strophes insofar as they don't rhyme or are less regular than I think of a stanza being. I tend to pick up a word, as in this poem in triads: "Daily as we are daily / wed, we say the world / is a wedding for which . . ." There is a complete triad, although it obviously isn't complete, the reader is forced on across the strophic break, but he's already been set up as I hear my own poem back, by the fact that "daily" occurs twice in the first line of the poem, and moves from initial position to terminal position in the line, an event that focuses, I would hope, subliminal attention to the fact that "wed" and "world" similarly function in the second line of the poem. So that something (beyond the delay of empty space) has to follow "is a wedding for which"— and, I hope, satisfy the possibility of "wedding"—even if here the parallel with the earlier lines turns out to be a kind of negative satisfaction. The way the poem works its rhythms in and across those two strophes, I hear as emphasized by what I take to be a very strong off-beat at the end of the first strophe. I hear that as certainly being analogous to jazz.

When you solve rhythmical problems in your poems, do they go a long way to solving content and sense problems? Do you revise by ear the way Oppen said he did?

Well, I never talked to George about how he did, and I've only recently read about him saying that he did, so I don't know. But I've mostly not been able to get a poem started until I got the rhythms right for my own ear in the first line. I seem to need to feel what the motion of the poem is going to be. And I think I probably try to teach this sort of thing as much as anything, now, in workshops. How a poem can pace itself, how a writer must be internally conscious of that pace; but I certainly don't think of it rationally in those terms. It's intuitive, but it comes from an ear that for me has moved in this wider course from the ear that I early had for assonance, consonance, rhyme, and so on.

In retrospect, do you find that when a poem is off rhythmically that it is also emotionally falsifying?

Well, I don't know that it's falsifying, that sounds too negative to me. I'd say that such a poem just hadn't found ways to express its emotion, to make its emotion move. Since I think of my monosyllables and rhythms as being comparatively hard-edged—to pick up on the jazz metaphor, not saxophone so much as they are trumpet—I do hear in my own work where a poem goes soft. When I feel a poem going soft it certainly often has to do with how the poem is moving. And rhythm is, of course, one function of how the poem is moving.

How did you arrive at—what seems to me new—a kind of staggered way of moving the poems, almost more than ever composing by phrase . . . ?

Well, there are two kinds of poems that are new in that respect. Poems like the title poem, "Relations . . . ," composed in stepped triads . . .

Though it doesn't look like that.

No, it doesn't look like that in proof but it might if the third and fourth lines were set just slightly further apart. There are earlier poems that were also composed with this same structure. "Poem for the Turn of the Century," and the poem "Generation," and another one called "Continuum" from *Before Sleep* (which I've dropped out of *Relations*), which was the first poem I wrote in this triadic stepped strophe. Though I like the stepped triad a lot, I wanted to get "Relations . . ." out of it once I started with it because I realized it was such a difficult-looking affair on the page. But the poem insisted on my continuing with it.

Then there are a whole series of other poems like "Eaton's Boatyard" or "North Haven" in which I hear the steps adding a dimension of "hold" to the run-on (if it exists) or a different beginning after an end-stop if that exists. So "composing by phrase" may be involved, in that the stepped part can be a whole phrase (like "clean of dreams" or "we have the weather" or "sipping long at the feeder"), but the possibility of stepping the line leaves me with one more option beyond a median caesura of some sort. As I hear these poems, I've added one more area of notation, to indicate to the reader that some movement is being changed.

In a stepped triad, where the lines tend to flow a little more freely and tend to be less punctuated in their own right than they are, say, in "Saying It," then I do hear the step as a notation that probably derives in part from a very open poem called "Lives" at the end of *Available Light*.

Would you be comfortable with the designation, formalist?

I don't mean to beg the question by saying that I don't think of myself in any particular terms, like formalist or absurdist. I do think that some of the poems I've written about work *are* about my sense of aesthetics. Like "Eaton's Boatyard," though I didn't realize it when I wrote it. "Building Her," too: the poem says I love the form that is appropriate to the action. And in "Dreamboat," which is basically a rather sexual poem about listening to jazz and wanting a boat and admiring a woman, all obviously interrelated, there's a little play in the middle of that, where I think of the woman as "a dreamboat built like a yawl *Concinnity*."

What does Concinnity mean?

I actually saw a yawl come in to Eaton's Boatyard once, and I didn't know what the name meant [*laughing*], so I asked the owner and he said look it up in the dictionary. It means "well built." [*Laughter.*] In that sense I like such structure as insists on its own right to be there. And is an enabling structure. As is the case with the hull of a good boat.

Before, in the earlier more highly formalistic poems—to use your word back—it seems to me too much was kept out of the poem; the poem too much insisted what began with A must thus go to B and thus go inevitably to C and so on. It was a formalism that I at one time needed. But I think the aleatory process of psychoanalysis, with a very good analyst who did not invite the slightest use of jargon, or in fact permit it, made all sorts of new ways of structuring available to me, insofar as I could let them come into my consciousness.

Are the new poems giving up some of that protective coloration you mentioned earlier in the conversation? That is, in what you now choose to let in to them?

When I was speaking of protective coloration I was thinking of the fact that I lead multiple lives, living here and also teaching at Syracuse, each as an escape route to another life. I take on a certain protective coloration here in order to go to the wharf and work on my boat. Which is entirely different from the kind of protective coloration I take on in Syracuse as a teacher, when I protect myself as a poet. I try to separate the poetry and the teaching as much as I can, and be as much as I can teacher rather than poet for students. I tend to start workshops by reminding students that I'm not their mother, father, lover, psychiatrist, rabbi, but will be their teacher if they let me be. And I say we both have to pretend that a teacher isn't, partially, all of those things. There's good sense in protecting oneself in order to be an effective teacher. By the same token, I try to keep some parts of my life utterly secret, except from the writing of them.

The whole notion of "letting in" fascinates me. For those of us who have over many years mostly written short poems, isn't there some thinking of closure that occurs, say mid-poem, where we get to a certain point and begin, almost by habit, to think of bringing the poem home . . . ? What I want to ask is, Does the "letting in" or the decision to "let in" occur around that time? Do most of us start to think too early about getting out of the poem?

You said "how we may get out of the poem." And that we feel the possibility of that closure coming, being mid-way. I think I don't feel it happening that way. I still don't know how long the poem is going to be, when it is at what proves to be its midway point. And I don't feel like getting *out* of the poem. I'm still trying to get down *into* the poem. When I get as far *in* as I can go—as with the poem you mentioned earlier, "Word": "I dug as deep as / my heart could stand"—then I know that I'm coming to the end of the poem and that it is coming to closure. And thus I must bring to bear whatever ways I know, intuitively, to feel my way through to closing the poem.

Can your heart stand more digging these days?

Some days, no, some nights, yes. [*Laughter.*] I don't think you can program it. All you can hope is that you can open yourself sufficiently to the experience not just of your own time (Justice Holmes, I think, said that a man must be open to the life of his times "at the peril of being judged not to have lived"), but you must open yourself as poet to the very age of your own life that you inhabit.

Let me take this a little bit further. There are not that many poets who write poetry of adulthood, who write adult poetry—it sounds silly to say it that way. Even in their later years so many poets are still talking about their childhoods, or the whatever of their pasts, anything but the conditions of their lives at that moment. It seems to me one of the things you've been able to do over the last ten years or so is to write about what it feels like to be alive in your own time with and among others.

I admire that very much in Williams, for example.

Yes, he would be an example.

And I admire it most of all in Yeats.

Isn't it more striking in Williams?

I think it is more striking. But I guess I'm remembering the poems of sexual yearning in Yeats, Yeats' rage for the absence of his own youth. And I think Hardy is just wonderful on passion, too. I think Hardy was very much an adult poet in this sense.

But even that yearning, in Yeats, is a kind of nostalgia, a nonconfrontation of the moment. . . .

That's nicely said. . . .

What is it, if you could say, to change the subject, that you find yourself most regretting, not in your life, but in your life as a poet? What would you like to have happened in the work—I'm not talking about fame or anything like that—what would you have wanted to happen in the work that may not have happened?

Oh I suppose I would have liked to learn more earlier. "The life so short, the art so long to learn." But I can't really regret, except that this poem isn't better, or that in that poem I didn't come closer. I've been astounded, making a book of *Relations,* at certain poems I've written. I cannot believe I wrote a particular poem, it comes so close to what I want a poem to be. They're very few, to be sure—but that they're there at all amazes me.

I used to feel "How do I get back to write that kind of poem?" One of the virtues of not reading in public is that one doesn't go back and read one's old poems very often, and so I'm quite often surprised at what I find I've written. Not always pleasantly, but often enough to keep going.

I've always liked Auden's remark that "a poet is never a poet except when he's writing a poem, the rest of the time he wishes he were." Given the world of capital *P*-Poetry now, I think that's an especially astute insight. I just received a folder from Poets & Writers the other day that says at the top "Writing doesn't have to be a solitary profession." Well, the hell it doesn't. [*Laughter.*] I think Poets & Writers is fine, but if they think that, they're off their rockers.

I don't mean to say that I have any definable sense of virtue or accomplishment or particular happiness about this or that aspect of my writing. But now and now again, when one person, and one person, and another person has written me to say a given poem has made a difference in how they feel about being alive, that means an immense amount to me.

I don't have any regrets about writing because I think one

can only, in the end, write as one must—somewhere close to the limits of one's own humanity. I don't think it's useful to have regrets. If I have regrets about my life—as we all do, I suppose—I know they are different from any possible regrets that I could have about writing, which is more controllable than one's life, and a sublimation in some way of one's losses. But as one speaks those losses clearly, is able to say them in the poems, they are somehow redeemed. Which reminds me how much I admire Jarrell, and how early I came to his poems called *Losses*. But I think the joy is in being able to make something that is sharable. . . .

Well, let's conclude by reading the title poem, which is the last poem in the book.

> *Relations: Old Light/New Sun/Postmistress/Earth/04421*
>
> From broken dreams,
>   we wake to every day's
> brave history,
>
> the gravity
>   of every moment
> we wake
>
> to let our lives
>   inhabit: now, here, again,
> this very day,
>
> passionate as all
>   Yeats woke in old age
> to hope for, the sun
>
> turns up, under
>   an offshore cloudbank
> spun at 700 and
>
> some mph to meet it,
>   rosy as the cheeks
> of a Chios woman
>
> Homer may have been
>   touched by, just
> as Janet

is touching, climbing
                    familiar steps, granite
locally quarried,

to work at 04421,
                    a peninsular village
spun, just as

Janet is spun,
                    into light, light appearing
to resurrect

not simply on its own
                    life but the whole
improbable

system, tugging
                    the planet around to
look precisely

as Janet looks,
                    alight with the gravity
of her office,

before turning
                    the key that opens up
its full

radiance:
            the familiar arrivals,
departures,

and even predictable
                    orbits in which,
with excited

constancy, by how
                    to each other
we're held, we keep

from spinning out
                    by how to each other
we hold.

Let me add one more thing about that. Again from Gelpi's book about Dickinson. A couple of nights ago I found him quoting from Emerson's "Representative Men": "Two cardinal facts lie forever at the base. The one and the two. One: unity or identity. Two: variety. Oneness and otherness. It is impossible to think or speak without embracing both." And Gelpi goes on with something that interests me a lot. "Man's perch, then, is at the fulcrum of a precarious see-saw." Strangely enough I find that echoing a line of my own from a serious-light poem, called "Adding It Up," in which I say "I see-saw on the old cliff . . . I think a lot of Saul Steinberg" [*laughter*]. Well, it seems to be that if the poems are precarious, in the good sense, it comes from an increased sense that it is impossible to speak or think without embracing both oneness and otherness. So the "I" of the poem in the course of the book *Relations* moves from being able to embrace only a word or two for naming a beach, as Adam does, to being able to embrace the otherness too, in that such embrace is absolutely requisite, an absolute fact of the world we inhabit. "By how / to each other / we're held, we keep from spinning out / by how to each other / we hold." So I think the entire curve of the book is from oneness to letting in the otherness. And, I hope, embracing the otherness.

UNDER DISCUSSION
Donald Hall, General Editor

Volumes in the Under Discussion series collect reviews and essays about individual poets. The series is concerned with contemporary American and English poets about whom the consensus has not yet been formed and the final vote has not been taken. Titles in the series include:

Please write for further information on available editions and current prices.

Ann Arbor

The University of Michigan Press